Vision Critical Studies

General Editor: Michael Egan

Wyndham Lewis:
Fictions and Satires

Vision Critical Studies published and in preparation:

Henry James: The Ibsen Years
The Silent Majority: A Study
of Working Class Fiction
E. E. Cummings
Margaret Drabble: Puritanism
and Permissiveness
The Fiction of Sex

WYNDHAM LEWIS: FICTIONS AND SATIRES

Robert T. Chapman

VISION

Vision Press Limited
157 Knightsbridge
London SW1X 7PA

ISBN 01 85478 362 8

187752

Printed in Great Britain
by Clarke, Doble & Brendon Ltd
Plymouth
MCMLXXIII

Contents

Editorial Note

Vision Critical Studies will examine mainly nineteenth-century and contemporary imaginative writing, delimiting an area of literary inquiry between, on the one hand, the loose generalities of the "reader's guide" approach and, on the other, the excessively particular specialist study. Crisply written and with an emphasis on fresh insights, the series will gather its coherence and direction from a broad congruity of approach on the part of its contributors. Each volume, based on sound scholarship and research, but relatively free from cumbersome scholarly apparatus, will be of interest and value to all students of the period.

M.E.E.

Acknowledgements

I am grateful to Mrs. Anne Wyndham Lewis, the widow of the writer, for permission to quote from the works of Wyndham Lewis in her copyright; to the Cornell University Library Board for permission to quote from their Lewis Archive; to Methuen and Co., for permission to quote from *The Letters of Wyndham Lewis* (Ed. W. K. Rose), *Tarr, The Art of Being Ruled, The Lion and the Fox, Time and Western Man, The Wild Body, Rotting Hill, The Writer and the Absolute, Self Condemned, The Demon of Progress in the Arts* and *The Human Age*; to Calder and Boyars Ltd., for permission to quote from *Blasting and Bombardiering*; to *Encounter* magazine for permission to quote from "Doppelgänger"; to Cassell and Co., for permission to quote from *Snooty Baronet* and *The Revenge for Love*; to the Hutchinson Publishing Group for permission to quote from *Rude Assignment*; to Hutchinson and the author for permission to quote from *The Georgian Literary Scene* by Frank Swinnerton; to The Hogarth Press and the Literary Estate of Leonard Woolf for permission to quote from his *Beginning Again*; to Hamish Hamilton Ltd., for permission to quote from *World Within World* by Stephen Spender; to Grey Arrow Publishers for permission to quote from *The Autobiography of Alice B. Toklas* by Gertrude Stein; to Macmillan and Co., for permission to quote from *The Letters of Edith Sitwell* (Eds. J. Lehmann and D. Parker); and to the Heinemann Group and the author for permission to quote from *Lytton Strachey* by Michael Holroyd.

Part of Chapter 5 of this book appeared in *Contemporary Literature* vol. 12, no. 2, Spring 1971, pp. 133–145. I am grateful to the Regents of The University of Wisconsin Press for permission to reprint.

Author's Note

Bracketed numbers after the quotations in the text refer to pages in first editions unless otherwise specified. Where a later edition has been used the date of this is given in the Selected Bibliography on pp. 186–188.

Preface

In the ferment of creativity that occurred at the beginning of this century, Pound, Joyce, Eliot and Lewis—"the men of 1914," as the latter called them—formed one crucial section of the imaginative writers who ushered the Modern Movement into Mr. Polly's England. Born of dissatisfaction with the traditional modes of expression, Modernism embodied a belief that if human character itself had not changed, then the means of apprehending it certainly had. Although the Modern Movement in literature shared no unifying "programme," there was a common desire to break away from the strictures of Edwardian realism represented by such figures as Wells, Bennett and Galsworthy. The twentieth century was a decade old before the Moderns, as T. S. Eliot said of Joyce, "killed the nineteenth century." Just as the geometrical Vorticist abstractions of Lewis communicate in a totally different way from the conventional realism of Sargent, for instance, so "The Enemy of the Stars" and *Tarr* reveal the abstract innovator in search of a new style of literary expression. "The greatest prose master of style of my generation," as Eliot called him, went on to develop a style that was as distinctively his own as his hard-edged draughtsmanship.

In the cultural history of the English *avant-garde*, Vorticism is of great significance in that it provided a rallying-point for like-minded artists, and *Blast*—Lewis's creation—is one of the essential documents of Modernism. With the same confidence that announced "The End of the Christian Era," Lewis proclaimed his Vorticist aesthetic and provided abstract designs and "The Enemy of the Stars" as evidence of an art that exalted space above time. The ideals he espoused, like the Classicism of T. E. Hulme and

9

the aesthetics of Worringer, rejected anthropocentric Greek and Roman art together with Romanticism in all its forms. The comparison with D. H. Lawrence, whom Lewis detested, shows these two writers at the opposite poles of Cartesian dualism, and their paintings reflect the fundamental dichotomy of their views. Lawrence's "Rape of the Sabine Women," for example, attempts to convey the tactile experience of soft, sensuous flesh; Lewis's portrait of Edith Sitwell, on the other hand, searches for the *form* beyond the flesh, and the sitter is reduced to a complex of hard, metallic, enduring surfaces. Similarly in their fiction, where Lawrence expresses the "carbon" of his character's being, that which lies beyond observation, Lewis concentrates upon the diamond exterior, the surface of the carapace, the behavioural patterns and the ideas that drive the man-machine.

Because his fiction is nearer that of Nashe and Smollett, his satires nearer Swift and Pope than the work of his contemporaries, it is difficult to assess Lewis's place in twentieth-century literature. Perhaps the comparison with Joyce is the most revealing. As Bernard Lafourcade has pointed out, Lewis provides an inverted mirror image of Joyce's major works: *Tarr* is the Lewisian portrait of the artist; *The Apes of God* his portrait of modern civilization (*Ulysses*); and *The Childermass* his lexical fantasy of a life-in-death wake-dream. Matching Joyce's technical daring, Lewis interprets the world in terms of the "Great Without"—the eye, the outside and space, as opposed to the ear, the inside and time—and his fiction of ideas is, as Ezra Pound said of *The Apes of God*, essential to the understanding of an important epoch in modern literature.

A belligerent social mask and "a tongue that naked goes" won Lewis many enemies during his lifetime, and the current journalistic snap-judgment about him tends to echo F. R. Leavis's cavalier dismissal of this "brutal and boring" writer. In *One-Way Song*, Lewis summed up his life-style in this way:

> Never has lived a week for twenty summers
> Free of the drumfire of camouflaged gunners,
> Never has eaten a meal that was undramatic—
> Without the next being highly problematic.
> Never succumbed to panic, *Kaltes blut*
> His watchword, facing ahead in untroubled mood.

> He has been his own bagman, critic, cop, designer,
> Publisher, agent, char-man and shoe shiner.

Lewis's reputation has always been overshadowed by the other "men of 1914," but many of his critics have suggested the imminence of a Lewis revaluation. Cyril Connolly, writing in *The Sunday Times* on March 30, 1969, points to one way in which his reputation could evolve:

> The Lewis lobby is now getting more influential, the attempt to get him into the Big Five (with Eliot, Joyce, Yeats and Pound as the Big Four) is gaining momentum. . . . Yeats, of course, is the wrong generation and only figures in conjunction with Pound. So in future will we talk about "Eliot, Joyce, Pound and Lewis"?

Connolly's question still remains unanswered and there is no consensus of opinion about this "man of dangerous vision," as he called himself. For years, Lewis has been a victim of the reductive fallacy: his total *oeuvre* has been seen in the light of its least attractive element, and his authoritarian politics have been accepted as the key to all his writing. Although Connolly's league-table is very much tongue-in-cheek, he does diagnose (and also, of course, helps create) a critical climate less likely to prejudge Lewis's imaginative writing on extra-literary grounds.

In his fiction, Lewis everywhere affirms the "superiority of live mind to dead mind" (Ezra Pound), and his best satires show him using the novel as a medium of polemics in a totally original way. Central to his theory and practice of fiction is the idea that art is "about something": transgressing many aesthetic principles and Flaubertian precepts, his writing is imbued with this philosophy. As a novelist, Lewis never achieved the formal beauty of *To the Lighthouse* or *A Passage to India*, and if, as F. R. Leavis has it, "depth, range, and subtlety in the presentment of human character" are the sole hallmarks of a great novelist, then Lewis is not of the elect. Lewis's aim—and his achievement—lie in a different direction. In *Men Without Art*, Lewis agrees with Henry James that the author's paramount duty is "the cure of souls": from this basic didactic premise proceeds a series of dialectical tourneys in which grotesque contestants, objective correlatives of equally grotesque philosophies, are slain by the rhetoric of the "Classical" Lewis-man. To evaluate such "thought adventures"

11

by the same criteria as one brings to Henry James or Virginia Woolf would be a mistake: this fiction of ideas—like a narrative *drame à thèse*—demands explication of a different order. Concentrating upon the dialectics of Lewis's imaginative writing, this chronological study sets out to define what is peculiarly "Lewisian" in these fictions and to elucidate some of their complex syllogistic patterns.

1

"Bagman, critic, cop, designer . . ." :
A literary life

Wyndham Lewis was born on his father's yacht on November 18th, 1882, when the boat of this "fox-hunting, brigantine-owning, essay-writing *bum*" (as Lewis called him in later years), was moored off Amherst, Nova Scotia. His mother was Anglo-Irish, his father an American who, wrote Lewis in *The Do-Nothing Mode*, "started life as a professional soldier. He became, at the end of his war-years, a professional idler . . . he was eccentric almost to the point of madness. Indeed, my mother affirmed that he was scarcely responsible for his actions, some of which departed so much from the norm as to be alarming." During his early youth Lewis "frisked and frollicked with other little American boys on the New England coast," and always seems to have been closer to his mother than to his father—the latter supplying, somewhat erratically, a much needed allowance after the parents' separation in 1893. Mother and son settled in London, and Lewis attended a succession of English schools, ending up at Rugby. Looking back on this part of his life, Lewis pointed to the part his flute-playing, dilettante father had played in his education:

> My father never made a cent in his life: the jack with which he paid my fees at an English Public School came from a silver spoon he found at birth stuck in his mouth by a good fairy: and if he *hadn't* been provided for in this fortunate manner I am positive he could never have made enough money to feed me let alone provide me with one of the most expensive and prolonged educations I have ever heard of. (*Letters*, 366–367)

Lewis left Rugby at the age of sixteen without distinguishing himself academically, but his true education was just beginning: "I did not go from Public School to University: Paris, where I went soon after Rugby, was my University."

The next ten years were Lewis's *wanderjahre* in Europe. Already acquainted with the art galleries of Paris, the young Lewis enjoyed a carefree and prolonged student-life on the Continent:

> Emerging from my schooldays, I found myself in the debilitating post-Nineties world of the first decade of the century. My views regarding politics were those of a young alligator. I had money in my pocket: not a great deal, but enough to live. I was given to understand I should always have money in my pocket—so I thought no more about economics, my own or other people's. I drifted into this relaxed and relaxing atmosphere and there was nothing at first to prick me into wakefulness. I tasted what people call perfect freedom therefore. There were no obstacles. Everything was easy: I was healthy: the mind slept like a healthy infant, in the sunlit smithy in which world war I was being hammered into shape. (*Rude Assignment*, 109)

From 1898–1901 he attended the Slade School of Art which nurtured some of the best artists of the day. The Slade not only developed Lewis's talents as a painter, but its intellectual *ethos* was evidently congenial to his literary bent. Known to his fellows as a "poet," Lewis recalls in *Rude Assignment* that he "began to write Petrarchan sonnets, but soon changed to Shakespearean. They were easier to do. Some were so like Shakespeare's that as I recall lines from them I am never quite certain whether they are Shakespeare's or mine." After leaving the Slade, Lewis travelled widely in Germany, France, Spain and Holland. Renting a studio in Paris—"the great humanist creation of the French"—he attended lectures by Bergson and, as *Tarr* reveals, soaked up the Parisian atmosphere. Next to the war, Paris was perhaps the greatest influence on the young Lewis's life. In *Rude Assignment* he recreates the excitement it held for him in these years:

> I went (to Paris) in its late sunset: its multitude of café-terraces swarmed with people from every corner of the earth: it was still *la nouvelle Athènes*, divinely disputatious. . . . It is dangerous to go to Heaven when you are too young. You do not understand it and

14

I did not learn to work in Paris. Many things, however, found their way into my mind as I moved about. First of all, I altered my appearance. Driven, by a vocational ferment, out of the British rut of snobbish sloth, I now became transformed, in contact with the Latin life, into something so different that had I a few years later encountered someone I had been to school with he would not have recognised me. I still went to a tailor in Brook Street for my clothes, but persuaded him to cut them into what must have seemed to his insular eye outrageous shapes. Gradually the bad effects of English education wore off, or were deliberately discarded. (113)

When it was intimated that his allowance was about to cease, Lewis returned to London in 1909 with the intention of making a living as a painter.

Almost immediately, he published some short stories in Ford Madox Hueffer's *The English Review*, and through Hueffer (later F. M. Ford) Lewis made contact with many young writers. The Tour Eiffel, The Old Chop House, the Café Royal, were favourite haunts of the intelligentsia, and Ford—in tails—would be dragged around such places by Lewis, Pound and others of "les jeunes" whose company he enjoyed. At this time, according to Ford in *Return to Yesterday*, "Lewis looked every inch a genius": immense steeple-crowned hat, long Russian overcoat, voluminous white silk cravat, hair parted at the centre and flopping onto his forehead, smoking incessantly; "he said not a word . . . I have never known anyone else whose silence was a positive rather than a negative quality." While his stories were appearing regularly, Lewis was also painting a good deal. Looking back on this early work, he saw himself "developing a mode of pictorial expression which was more 'advanced' than that of other people at that time." He first exhibited his work with the Camden Town Group in 1911; the reaction from *The Times* could not have been very encouraging: "Mr. Wyndham Lewis exhibits three geometrical experiments which many people will take for bad practical jokes."

A year before Lewis first exhibited, from November 1910 to January 1911, Roger Fry's famous Post-Impressionist show at the Grafton Galleries had caused an uproar. As Virginia Woolf wrote in *Roger Fry*, the public had responded with "paroxysms of rage and laughter. They went from Cézanne to Gauguin, from Gauguin to Van Gogh, they went from Picasso to Segonzac, from Derain to

15

Friez, and they were infuriated." A second, even more radical Post-Impressionist Exhibition opened on October 5th, 1912, again at the Grafton. Most established artists refused to co-operate, but Lewis exhibited alongside many young, *avant-garde* English experimentalists.

Lewis was very receptive to ideas he saw being tried out on the Continent and, as Walter Michel has suggested, his "Theatre Manager" (1909) "may be the first picture outside Paris to show a knowledge of the 'Demoiselles d'Avignon.'" Similarly, he absorbed the influence of Kandinsky as early as 1913 and was certainly one of the earliest abstractionists in England at a time when, according to the critic of *The Times*, "most people meant by Post-Impressionist pictures pictures which anyone could paint if he chose." The fight against philistine rejection of artistic experiment was the first of many polemical tournaments in which Lewis was to engage, and although he had not yet indulged in public art-politics, he appears to have been active backstage: "Impatient of quietude, star-gazing, or wool-gathering," writes Augustus John in *Chiaroscuro*, "our new Machiavelli sought to ginger up his friends, or patients as they might be called, by a whisper here, a dark suggestion there." John presents Lewis as a wild, mysterious figure, playing the part of "an incarnate Loki, bearing the news and sowing discord with it." Lewis's apprentice-ship in what he called "artistic power politics" culminated in the founding of Vorticism and the publication of *Blast*. As a result of the *mêlée* which surrounded these two events, Lewis found, much to his surprise, that "from a position of relative obscurity (he) became extremely well known."

The Omega affair (see "The Malefic Cabal") set Lewis at odds with a very powerful section of the Establishment art-world in England. As a direct result of the break with Fry in November 1913, Lewis became friendly with C. R. W. Nevinson. Together the young artists decided to arrange a dinner in honour of F. T. Marinetti, the Italian Futurist, who was scouring the country looking for disciples. Marinetti had been visiting England inter-mittently since 1910, flamboyantly haranguing any meeting that would listen to him. The small volatile Italian, "adorned with diamond rings, gold chains and hundreds of flashing white teeth," lectured so vehemently and with such an impassioned torrent of words, that, according to *The Times*, "some of his audience begged for mercy." At first Lewis seemed to fall under the spell of the Italian, and in an article in *The New Weekly* entitled "A Man of the Week: Marinetti," he praised the "intellectual Cromwell of our time" for the inspiration he had given to English artists: "England has needed these foreign auxiliaries to put her energies to rights and restore order. Marinetti's services, in this home of aestheticism, crass snobbery, and languors of distinguished phlegm, are great." But Lewis was never long a disciple, and the only occasion on which he was happy as part of a group was when he happened to lead it: the break with Marinetti was soon to come.

In March 1914, with financial help from Kate Lechmere, Lewis had founded The Rebel Art Centre in Great Ormond Street, within sniping distance of the heart of Bloomsbury. Although the Centre was shortlived, it provided an important focal point for like-minded English artists, including Wadsworth, Nevinson, Gaudier-Brzeska, Bomberg and Epstein, and writers such as Pound, Ford and T. E. Hulme. As an educational establishment, however, it was a failure: "a man who desired to improve the design of gas brackets, and a lady pornographer" were their only students. Yet, among others, Marinetti lectured there, and it was from the Centre's address that he and Nevinson issued their "Futurist Manifesto: Vital English Art," a typical Futurist attack on "passéisme," which was printed in *The Observer* on June 7th, 1914. The Manifesto rehearsed familiar Futurist themes, which Lewis had endorsed in his "Man of the Week" article the previous month. Marinetti and Nevinson declared themselves "AGAINST":

> The pessimistic, sceptical and narrow views of the English public, who stupidly adore the pretty-pretty, the commonplace, the soft, sweet, and mediocre, the sickly revivals of mediaevalism, the Garden Cities with their curfews and artificial battlements, the Maypole Morris dances, Aestheticism, Oscar Wilde, the Pre-Raphaelites, Neo-primitives and Paris.

They were for, among other things, "motors," "sport," and the creation of a powerful *avant-garde* of artists to act as

> an exciting stimulant, a violent incentive for creative genius, a constant inducement to keep alive the fires of invention and of art,

so as to obviate the monotonous labour and expense of perpetual raking out and relighting of the furnace.

Nevinson was a valuable propagandist for Futurism in England, and he followed in the master's exuberant footsteps, taking copies of the Manifesto to theatres and scattering them from "the gods" to the stalls. The publication of the Manifesto was the signal for the secession of Lewis and others who, while endorsing some of the premises of Futurism, did not consider themselves part of the movement. The Manifesto had mentioned Lewis and several of the Rebel Art Centre group as "the great Futurist painters or pioneers and advance forces of vital English Art," and so Lewis wrote to *The Observer* dissociating himself from the Manifesto. *The Daily Express* (June 11th) noted that "the dynamic leader of the Italian futurists had put his hand into a wasps' nest in issuing his latest manifesto": the schism was made more obvious at the Doré Gallery next day where Marinetti was to lecture and Nevinson read the Manifesto. Lewis describes the counter-putsch in *Blasting and Bombardiering*:

> I assembled in Greek Street a determined band of anti-futurists. Mr. Epstein was there; Gaudier-Brzeska, T. E. Hulme, Edward Wadsworth and a cousin of his called Wallace, who was very muscular and forcible, according to my eminent colleague, and he rolled up very silent and grim. There were about ten of us. After a hearty meal we shuffled bellicosely round to the Doré Gallery.
>
> Marinetti had entrenched himself upon a high lecture platform, and he put down a tremendous barrage in French as we entered. Gaudier went into action at once. He was very good at the *parlez-vous*, in fact he was a Frenchman. He was sniping at him without intermission, standing up in his place in the audience all the while. The remainder of our party maintained a confused uproar. (33)

Fireworks were set off, the heckling was non-stop; next day, *The Manchester Guardian* announced the secession from Futurism of "Messrs. Wyndham Lewis and Co., who now call themselves Vorticists."

Futurism was important in the genesis of Vorticism in that it gave a well-defined aesthetic stimulus against which "Lewis and Co." could react. By June 1914, the Marinetti personality cult was itself beginning to seem decidedly *passé*. On the day after the

Doré Gallery fracas, *The Times* reported a parody by Sir Arthur Quiller-Couch in the *Cambridge Magazine*, which "should kill Futurism, if indeed Futurism is not a thing of the past." By 1914 Futurism had become an old joke, and was being characterized by the press as the ordinary, the everyday, masquerading as the profound, merely by shouting loudly. As *The Times* critic put it: "The public is interested in the Futurists because they explain themselves so volubly. . . . A chocolate-box picture remains one, even if you cut it up into little pieces and then shuffle them."

The Rebel Art Centre formed the kernel of the *Blast* group and Vorticism, and this new movement replaced Futurism as the journalistic talking point in the arts: "By August 1914 no newspaper was complete without news about 'Vorticism' or its arch-exponent Mr. Lewis," wrote the arch-exponent himself. Looking back on this era more than twenty years later, Lewis analysed the cultural forces which had created this phenomenon:

> The Press in 1914 had no Cinema, no Radio, and no Politics: so the painter could really become a "star" . . . oil paintings were "news." Exhibitions were reviewed in column after column. And no illustrated paper worth its salt but carried a photograph of some picture of mine or of my "school," as I have said, or one of myself, smiling insinuatingly from its pages. (*Blasting and Bombardiering*, 36)

Although the term "Vortex"—the still point of creation—was Ezra Pound's, the latter conceded that Lewis "certainly made Vorticism." The movement never developed anything approaching a coherent aesthetic philosophy; it was, rather, a collection of predilections summarily unified by a common "style." Lewis was the driving force behind it, and there is much truth in his disputed claim, in the catalogue of the 1956 Tate retrospective, that "Vorticism, in fact, was what I, personally, did, and said, at a certain period."

Lewis was now spending "50 per cent of (his) time in propaganda and similar activities," yet he was still carrying out some important work. He completed murals for the "Cave of the Golden Calf," Soltyk's "Tour Eiffel" restaurant, and created a "Cubist Room" at Lady Drogheda's London home with jet black floor and ceiling, and black velvet walls hung with his own paintings.

Exhibiting with different "Groups," he was always very aware of the sociology of the art-world, and even before Vorticism crystallized into a movement, Lewis had been conscious of affinities between certain artists who showed specifically "English" traits, rather than the Latinate associations of Futurism.

The publication of *Blast* in July 1914 gave this new movement a voice and a rallying point. Lewis was the editor and major contributor to this "puce monster" with the dimensions of a telephone directory: "No more high-brow publication," he wrote in *Blasting and Bombardiering*, "ever saw the light in England." Lewis's opening statement is typical of the elliptical and ironical style of the Manifestos:

> Long live the great art vortex sprung up in the centre of this town.
> We stand for the Reality of the Present—not the sentimental Future or the sacripant Past. . . .
> We do not want to make people wear Futurist patches, or fuss men to take to pink and sky blue trousers. . . .
> AUTOMOBILISM (Marinetteism) bores us. We do not want to go about making a hulla-baloo about motor cars, anymore than about knives and forks, elephants or gas pipes. . . .
> The Futurist is a sensational and sentimental mixture of the aesthete of 1890 and the realist of 1870. (8)

Gaudier's "Vortex" concentrates upon sculptural values, and Pound, applying synaesthetically the basic concept of Imagist poetry to all the arts, talks of the Vorticist using only the "primary pigments" of the medium of expression in which he works. Lewis later referred disparagingly to Pound's contribution as "Chinese Crackers, and a trayful of mild jokes," but some of Pound's poems, especially *Salutation the Third*, rise to the same heights of violent invective as Lewis's own pieces:

> Let us deride the smugness of "The Times":
> GUFFAW!
> So much the gagged reviewers,
> It will pay them when the worms are wriggling in their vitals;
> These were they who objected to newness,
> HERE are their TOMB-STONES.
> They supported the gag and the ring;

A little black box contains them.
so shall you be also,
You slut-bellied obstructionist;
You sworn foe to free speech and good letters,
You fungus, you continuous gangrene. . . .
I have seen many who go about with supplications,
Afraid to say how they hate you.
HERE is the taste of my BOOT,
CARESS it, lick off the BLACKING. (45)

The most impressive performance in *Blast* was undoubtedly
Lewis's own "Vorticist drama," "The Enemy of the Stars." Allusive,
imagist stage-directions create the ambience of this super-real
drame à thèse in which the two antagonists, Hanp and Arghol,
are destined to enact their eternal bloody conflict. This timeless
world is alien and elemental:

The Earth has burst, a granite flower, and disclosed the scene.
A wheelwright's yard.
Full of dry, white volcanic light.
Full of emblems of one trade: stacks of pine, iron, wheels stranded.
Rough Eden of one soul, to whom another man, and not EVE, would
be mated.
A canal at one side, the night pouring into it like blood from a
butcher's pail.
Rouge mask in aluminium mirror, sunset, grimace through the night.
A leaden gob, slipped at zenith, first drop of violent night, spreads
cataclysmically in harsh water of Evening. Caustic Reckett's stain.
Three trees, above canal, sentimental, black and conventional in
number, drive leaf flocks, with jeering cry. (62)

Stripped of inessential words, this jagged, primitive style is harsh
to the ear, conveying excellently the sparse brutality of the setting.

Hanp and Arghol are representative figures: Hanp of a dull-
witted and violent "Mankind," hating Arghol because he senses
him to be somehow "different." Unlike his fellow, Arghol is
endowed with reason, intellectual, well-travelled and worldly-wise.
The struggle between Hanp and Arghol is a symbolic one, and
the conflict it represents is present in much of Lewis's work: it is
that between the one and the many, the artist and the world, the
individual and the crowd, Natures and Puppets, or—as defined in
the play—"Personality and Mankind." As a sighted man amongst

21

the blind, Arghol is hated for his vision and made to feel guilt for his uniqueness; yet, however much he tries, he cannot escape his destiny. Life, he sees, is nasty, brutish and short, and he is very much aware of its inherent absurdity: Hanp, on the other hand, merely endures it. The play weighs the relative burden and value of this gift of knowledge.

"In the crowd, yet not of the crowd" is Lewis's concept of the ideal position of the artist in society. "The Enemy of the Stars," in one sense, is a metaphysical definition of this role and a denial of its existential possibility. Because he comes into contact with Hanp-Mankind, Arghol is destined to become "Arghol"—a mass-produced *persona*, a false self, a crowd creation—from which he cannot escape:

> The process and condition of life, without any exception, is a grotesque degradation, and "souillure" of the original solitude of the soul. There is no help for it, since each gesture and word partakes of it, and the child has already covered himself with mire. Anything but yourself is dirt. (70)

Philosophical awareness of the predicament does not, however, bring consolation. Arghol sees that his individuality is a gesture of defiance against the cosmic—as well as the human—way of the world: in this sense he is "The Enemy of the Stars," whose destiny is "an extremely unpleasant one" (70). Existence militates against individuality, and the anonymous, inhuman beatings endured by Arghol as the play opens symbolize the unwillingness of life to tolerate a Personality:

> The figure rushed without running. Arghol heeled over to the left. A boot battered his right hand ribs. These were the least damaged: it was their turn.

> Upper lip shot down, half covering chin, his body reached methodically. At each blow, in muscular spasm, he made the pain pass out. Rolled and jumped, crouched and flung his grovelling Enceladus weight against it, like swimmer and wave. (63)

This pattern of violence is echoed, on the personal plane, in Arghol's relationship with Mankind. Hanp questions him about the wonders of the world. He seeks dreams, but Arghol gives him a disillusioned vision of existence, and Hanp is unable to bear so much reality. As they fight, the universe mocks them in violent acts of pathetic fallacy:

> The great beer-coloured sky, at the fuss, leapt in fete of green gaiety.
>
> Its immense lines bent like whalebones and sprang back with slight deaf thunder. . . .
>
> The bleak misty hospital of the horizon grew pale with fluid of anger. . . .
>
> The attacker rushed in drunk with blows. They rolled, swift, jagged rut, into one corner of shed: large insect scuttling roughly to hiding. . . .
>
> Hanp fell somewhere in the shadow: there lay.
>
> Arghol stood rigid. . . .
>
> His mind, baying mastiff, he flung off.
>
> In steep struggle he rolled into sleep. (75–76)

Arghol will not pander to Hanp: he refuses to become "Arghol" and be thus assimilated into a mankind intent on extinguishing all signs of excellence. The tragedy moves inexorably to its conclusion: Hanp murders Arghol ("the knife sliced heavily the impious meat"), and finally commits suicide:

> He sprang from the bridge clumsily, too unhappy for instinctive science, and sank like lead, his heart a sagging weight of stagnant hatred. (85)

Looking back on *Blast*, Lewis later wrote that it was, "as its name implies, destructive in intention. What it aimed at destroying . . . was . . . the 'academic' of the Royal Academy tradition." In his work of demolition Lewis did not use the ground-rules of the academics, but went beyond the conventions of civilized debate, employing the rhetoric of "flyting." The personal abuse contained in the pages of *Blast* is, however, a means to an end: it is an attempt to shock the aesthetically staid, while also acting as a rallying-point for the *avant garde*. The "Blasts and Blesses"

23

are a series of elliptical curses or cheers for diverse facets of contemporary culture. The "Blasts," "Damns," and "Curses" are half an inch tall, and the inventive typography is reminiscent of the ideographical experiments of *Lacerba* and Apollinaire's *L'antitradition futuriste* (June 1913), which contained a series of "Merde aux . . ." and "Rose aux . . .", antedating Lewis's "Blasts and Blesses" by about a year. The Blasting of France is fairly typical of the tone of Lewis's pronouncements:

OH BLAST FRANCE

PIG PLAGIARISM

BELLY

SLIPPERS

POODLE TEMPER

BAD MUSIC

SENTIMENTAL GALLIC GUSH

SENSATIONALISM

FUSSINESS

PARISIAN PAROCHIALISM (13)

About fifty individuals are also selected for personal blasts, they include "The Bishop of London and all his posterity. Galsworthy . . . Bergson . . . Beecham (Pills, Opera, Thomas)," and other representatives of the inimical *status quo*. "I am all in favour of a young man behaving rudely to everyone in sight," wrote Lewis in later years. "This may not be good for the young man, but it's good for everyone else."

As a quick aesthetic shock-therapy treatment, *Blast*'s invective did not have quite the desired revolutionary effect on one reader at least. The critic of *The Times* reviewed the periodical on July 1st, 1914:

The fine frenzy of the authors of *Blast* has made havoc of its printing press, and we do not remember seeing in a publication of its size so many misprints . . . the reader may make what he can . . . of a great many papal statements about art, life, nature, the present, the past, the future, and other matters; of some poetry by Mr. Ezra Pound—of no particular merit, and some of no merit at all; of some fiction by Ford Madox Hueffer and Rebecca West, and above all of a number of cartoons, or rather diagrams, of the type now familiar with those who take any interest in the artistic "isms," and among which Mr. Wyndham Lewis's "Portrait of an

24

Englishwoman" might—outside the vortex—easily change titles with Mr. Wadsworth's "Cape of Good Hope." (8)

The "diagrams" to which *The Times'* critic takes exception are among the earliest abstract drawings executed by English artists. Some of Lewis's are geometrically violent designs, the violence of which is expressed by angular lines and the interplay of diagonals with verticals, rather than by the "subject matter."

The month after the first issue of *Blast* appeared, England declared war on Germany: the "big bloodless brawl, prior to the Great Bloodletting" was over, and the bloodletting proper began. Gaudier-Brzeska contributed to the second issue of *Blast* an article on the Vortex, "written from the trenches." The same issue contained his obituary. Lewis did not immediately enlist—he was troubled by an intermittent illness which laid him low for months at a time—and he used this period of enforced idleness to complete his first novel (*Tarr*) and to carry on painting. The outcome of this spell of painting was seen in the first Vorticist Exhibition in June 1915, at the Doré Galleries. Lewis's introduction to the catalogue was in the tone of his *Blast* writings: pouring scorn upon the "sugary, cheap, anecdotal and in every way pitiable muck poured out by the ton," he stated the positives of Vorticism to be "Activity," "Significance," and "Essential Movement." The second *Blast* came out a month later and contained poems and articles by Pound, and poems by T. S. Eliot. Lewis hopefully announced two future numbers (which never appeared), and proudly reprinted remarks by hostile critics about the first issue's "irrepressible imbecility." Pound, mocking at the mockery, barked back:

> The common or homo canis snarls violently at the thought of there being ideas which he doesn't know. He dies a death of lingering horror at the thought that even after he has learned even the newest set of made ideas, that the horrid things will grow, will go on growing in spite of him. (86)

Lewis's hopes for the future were great: "We have subscribers in the Khyber Pass, and subscribers in Santa Fé. The first stone in the world-wide reformation of taste has been securely laid." This reformation, however, was to be yet another casualty of the war: it "had washed out the bright puce of the cover of the organ of the 'Great London Vortex.' Too much blood had been shed for red, even of the most shocking aniline intensity, to startle anybody."

Lewis was obviously in no hurry to enlist in the army. He attempted to secure a none too hazardous position since, as he put it, "I have as little reason to be shot . . . as any artist in Europe." He offered his "accomplishments" to the war-effort, rather than his right arm, which was, he wrote, more "a creative than a destructive limb." Finally, he volunteered in March 1916, was commissioned by Christmas, in France by May 1917, and served at the front for about seven months. Although Lewis escaped serious injury, his friend T. E. Hulme was killed in a neighbouring battery. Lewis's war experiences are recounted with grim humour in *Blasting and Bombardiering* where, with racy understatement, he captures the tone of wartime as surely as in his paintings:

> In the morning the battery usually stank of sweet gas. Men were always going sick. A gunner who got down into a shell hole, where the gas clung for hours, was laid out. We kept them out of holes if we could.
>
> For weeks on end every man in the battery slept in his gas mask. In lying down we fixed our gas masks with the tin teat just up against our lips. Before we were all asleep one of us—usually Boorfelt—would sit up and say "gas!" Then we stuck our tin teats in our mouths, and clipped the pincers on our noses. So we would sleep for the rest of the night. (143)

At the beginning of 1918 Lewis became an official war artist for the Canadian War Records Office. Leaving his "squalid, insanitary, little rat-hole" at the front, he again took up his brushes to "bring to life upon the canvas a painted battery." These paintings were exhibited in February 1919 at the Goupil Gallery under the title "Guns by Wyndham Lewis." In the catalogue Lewis stated that he had waived experimentation in the attempt to give "a personal and immediate expression of a tragic event"; Walter Michel has suggested that these paintings are "possibly the best of World War I in any country."

The war transformed Lewis's outlook on life and also upon art:

The war was a sleep, deep and animal, in which I was visited by images of an order very new to me. Upon waking I found an altered world: and I had changed, too, very much. The geometrics which had interested me so exclusively before, I now felt were bleak and empty. They wanted *filling*. They were still as much present to my mind as ever, but submerged in the coloured vegetation, the flesh and blood that is life. (*Rude Assignment*, 129)

Vorticism was a thing of the past; the "great bloodletting" had changed the world of art dramatically. It had not only robbed Lewis of some of his closest friends, but it had caused a hiatus in his life to which it was difficult to adjust. "Starting all over again," Lewis founded "Group X," a loosely-knit group of ten artists, some of whom had been friends in the *Blast* days. They held their first exhibition in March 1920. In his foreword to the Mansard Gallery catalogue, Lewis makes the point that each exhibitor "sails his own boat, and may lift his sails to any wind that may seem to him to promise a prosperous cruise." In other words, there was no sense of purpose common to all, and they soon disbanded: "I left this Group," wrote Lewis, "and it fell to pieces."

After 1920 Lewis divorced himself from further group activity; he still engaged in art politics, but as an outsider—a man alone. W. K. Rose, in *The Letters*, perceptively analyses the changes in Lewis's literary "selves":

Since a part of Lewis flourished in the limelight, it is not surprising that he should have worked out a solution to the dilemma created by this growing singleness and privacy. A public image appeared in his writing and drawing and began to lead a dual life with the private person. Wyndham Lewis left the stage to "Mr. Wyndham Lewis," The Tyro, The Enemy. The personae themselves were given a variety of masks. (122)

The Tyro was the title of the second little magazine which Lewis founded and edited. The first issue, (it only ran to two), was published in April 1921, and the same month saw the opening of Lewis's exhibition "Tyros and Portraits." Great grinning automata, Lewis's Tyros are, like grotesque seaside postcard caricatures, parodies of humanity. He described the Tyros in his foreword to the Leicester Galleries exhibition:

These immense novices brandish their appetites in their faces, lay bare their teeth in a valedictory, inviting, or merely substantial laugh. A laugh, like a sneeze, exposes the nature of the individual that is perhaps a little unreal. This sunny commotion in the face, at the gate of the organism, brings to the surface all the burrowing and interior broods which the individual may harbour.

The laugh of the Tyro exposes the body's mechanism; it reveals a person behaving as a thing—the nature of comedy for Lewis.

Lewis entitled his review *The Tyro* not simply because he wished to adopt the *persona* of an "Elemental," but because here the Tyros would reveal both themselves and the stupidities of the age. Lewis himself, in prophetic style, heralds a "New Epoch" which must break away from the clutches of the past if it is to fulfil its potential:

> The advocates of the order that we supersede are still in a great majority. The obsequies of the dead period will be protracted, and wastefully expensive. But it is nevertheless nailed down, cold, but with none of the calm and dignity of death. The post-mortem has shown it to be suffering from every conceivable malady. (3)

Symptomatic of the malady are the aesthetics of Bloomsbury and, more particularly, of Lewis's old enemy Roger Fry. Lewis saw the "honoured leader" as a powerful arbiter of public taste, whose aesthetic predilections were "saturated with William Morris's prettiness and fervour, 'Art for Art's sake,' late Victorianism"—everything, in fact, which held back the New Epoch. Although *The Tyro* had been advertised as appearing "at intervals of two or three months," the second issue (like *Blast* No. 2) did not appear for almost a year. Bloomsbury, the Royal Academy, Romanticism, and dilettante aesthetes, are again the villains of the piece, and all the *Tyro* contributors are united in attempting to create different aesthetic criteria to those of the current artistic Establishment.

Although Lewis was at the centre of intellectual life after the war—he kept up his friendship with Eliot and Pound, for instance—he began, more and more, to cut himself off from fashionable socio-intellectual circles. Less involved in the propaganda of art-politics, Lewis was "incubating and pretty silent," and the early years of the twenties were a period of intense reading and writing. Like all literary men without a private income, he was often troubled by the want of pence. He remarked on the problem in *Rude Assignment*: "What can the . . . gifted man without income do? He can save up, retire to an inexpensive spot, budget for what is usually an inadequate period, with one packet of cigarettes a week and two pints of beer on Saturday evenings." When some of Lewis's wealthier admirers set up a fund to help him, he was able to "go underground" and follow his own predilections without worrying about pot-boiling. Freed from the necessity of "playing the boiled shirt game" of "lunching, dining, cocktailing" in Mayfair, he got through an "unspeakable amount of work."

One of the products of this period "underground" was a series of books which, as Roy Campbell has said, "traverse the literature of the first half of this century like a range of Himalayas." Between 1926 and 1930, Lewis published four major works: *The Art of Being Ruled* (1926) and *Time and Western Man* (1927) deal with the philosophy of politics and the politics of "time" philosophies; *The Childermass* (1928) and *The Apes of God* (1930) —embodying in fiction many of the ideas presented discursively in these earlier works—are, as Ezra Pound said, "essential to an understanding of a twenty-year English epoch." In *The Art of Being Ruled*, Lewis is well aware that he is swimming against that tide of accepted ideas which he labelled "english liberalism," and his book "must make its own audience; for it aims at no audience already there with which I am acquainted." Brilliant insights into "the will that finds expression in the doctrines of our contemporaries" vie for place of honour with inveterate and idiosyncratic attacks upon such topics as the "prevalent Shamanistic fashion" (homosexuality) and the nature of Woman. The basic premise which informs Lewis's political argument is that the vast majority of people are incapable of deciding by whom, or how, they should be governed. The "herd" has a "profound instinct" to be ruled, and it is the intellectual's *responsibility*, he postulates, to organize society. Political analysis gives way to prescriptive sociology as Lewis cavalierly lays down the law for those "being ruled." However philosophically and "aesthetically" valid these neo-platonic ideas may or may not be, when translated into political reality they cannot solely be judged *qua* ideas. The Ideal State which emerges is like a Neo-Classical Utopia—albeit without the Catholicism—in which a "despotic, or at all events, very powerful, control" is accepted as a necessity. In *The Art of Being Ruled*, Lewis brings the mind of an artist-philosopher to the practical realities of politics and, like an autocratic Caliph, designs a society in which "the good ruler" and "the good artist" come together—as in Plato's *Republic*.

The year after *The Art of Being Ruled* was published, Lewis launched his third magazine, *The Enemy*. He had obviously learned not to be too optimistic about the frequency of his periodicals, the opening words of the magazine stress this point: "It is regrettable that this paper cannot be definitely advertised as a quarterly; but although that is what will be aimed at, no guarantee can be given as to its punctual appearance." His editorial defines his critical stance: Lewis is outside all movements—"a solitary outlaw and not a gang. . . . Outside I am freer." Again and again, Lewis assures his readers that he owes no allegiance to any individual or ideology and that his observations will thus "contain no social impurities whatever; there will be nobody with whom I shall be dining tomorrow night (of those who come within the scope of my criticism) whose susceptibilities, or whose wife's, I have to consider." From this basic attitude Lewis develops the more comprehensive *persona* of "The Enemy," and a great sense of seriousness behind the belligerent mask is everywhere apparent: "The names we remember in European literature are those of men who satirized and attacked, rather than petted and fawned upon, their contemporaries. Only *this* time exacts an uncritical hypnotic sleep of all within it."

Lewis contributed more than ninety per cent of the material to the three issues of the magazine. Each edition contains a very long, almost book-length, contribution from him. The first of these is "The Revolutionary Simpleton," which aims to "contradict, and if possible defeat" the current notions of "time" both at their genesis in philosophy, and as they are popularized in literature, (this was later incorporated into *Time and Western Man*.) As always, Lewis makes clear his own position at the outset: "It is the criticism of this view, the time view, from the position of the plastic or the visual intelligence, that I am submitting to the public in this book." Lewis sees "time-philosophy" as a species of Romanticism; it concentrates upon the otherworldly, to the neglect—indeed the denial—of the "classical," rational values. The "Revolutionary Simpleton" is sick for things he has never experienced, and Lewis, with characteristically sardonic wit, uses Ezra Pound as prime example. Pound, argues Lewis, is forever on the lookout for something new, something sensational, change for its own sake, and is a passive follower of *avante-garde* fashion:

> It is *disturbance* that Pound requires; that is the form his parasitism takes. He is never happy unless he is sniffing the dust and glitter of *action* kicked up by other, more natively "active," men. . . . Pound is, I believe, only pretending to be alive for form's sake. His effective work seems finished. (63)

In following these latest encyclicals of fashion, Pound is, according to Lewis, a "genuine *naif*." Gertrude Stein, on the other hand, is "not the real article," but a *faux naif*. "Trudy" has *cultivated* her childish language and mannerisms: "she is not simple at all, although she writes usually so like a child—like a confused, stammering, rather 'soft' (bloated, acromegalic, squinting and spectacled, one can figure it as) child." In editorials Lewis often denied that he had "anything to do with personalities," being concerned solely with ideas, but his treatment of Gertrude Stein totally destroys this disclaimer. His polemical assaults are enlivened by incisive asides which, while not always concerned with "ideas," contribute greatly to a very lively argument: in playing her literary game, writes Lewis, Gertrude Stein "may be described as the reverse of Patience sitting on a monument—she appears, that is, as a Monument sitting upon Patience." Her "prose-song," too, is witheringly dissected in a manner which ridicules as it analyses:

> Gertrude Stein's prose-song is a cold, black, suet-pudding. We can represent it as a cold suet-roll of fabulously reptilian length. Cut it at any point, it is the same thing; the same heavy, sticky, opaque mass all through, and all along. It is weighted, projected, with a sybylline urge. It is mournful and monstrous, composed of dead and inanimate material. It is all fat without nerve. Or the evident vitality that informs it is vegetable rather than animal. Its life is a low-grade, if tenacious, one; of the sausage, by-the-yard, variety. (82)

31

Because *Ulysses* is a "time book," Joyce also comes in for a devastating salvo from the "Lewis gun." He is seen as part of the Bergson-Einstein, Stein-Proust, "Time School," whose concentration upon the subjective renders redundant the enduring verities Lewis espouses. Joyce's technique, Lewis believes, has affinities with Trudy's "gargantuan mental stutter":

> This habit of speech, like a stuttering infection is very contagious. Mr. Joyce even has caught it; and, one of the most pedagogically careful of men, has thrown overboard a great deal of laboriously collected cargo, and romps along at the head of the fashionable literary world, hand in hand with Gertrude Stein, both outdoing all children in jolly quaintness. (74)

Not all Lewis's criticism is in this bantering tone: his critique of Whitehead, Spengler and Alexander as time philosophers is erudite without, however, being dryly academic or solemn, and a strand of irony runs throughout the polemics of "The Revolutionary Simpleton."

Accompanying Lewis's impressive piece in this first issue are T. S. Eliot on "Poetry and Belief," W. Gibson on Chirico's paintings, and J. W. N. Sullivan on the nature of music. They are merely curtain-raisers before Lewis's *pièce de résistance*, and in *The Enemy* he seems less concerned with providing a platform for like-minded writers, and more with providing one for his own "occasional" polemical pieces. *The Enemy*, however, was not a financial success. Lord and Lady Waterhouse, friends of Lewis, backed the venture which lost £450 on the first two issues. The first *Enemy* was widely praised; the *Times Literary Supplement* called "The Revolutionary Simpleton" "the finest and most searching piece of literary criticism we have had for a long while." The second issue appeared in September 1927, and was devoted to Lewis's "Pale-face"—the only other article being an abstruse interpretation of some of Lewis's arguments from the point of view of Roman Catholic teaching.

"Paleface" is the study of the attitudes underlying certain works of contemporary literature which are represented by Lawrence's *Mornings in Mexico* and Sherwood Anderson's *Dark Laughter*:

I wish to stress, then, that these essays do not come under the heading of "literary criticism." They are written purely as investigations into contemporary states of mind, as these are displayed for us by imaginative writers pretending to give us a picture of current life "as it is lived," but who in fact give us much more of a picture of life as, according to them, it *should* be lived. (5)

Lewis saw the glorification of the mystical, dark races (as opposed to the rational spirit of the white consciousness), as an abdication of the reason in favour of the unconscious. "I would rather have an ounce of human consciousness," Lewis writes, "than a universe full of 'abdominal' afflatus and hot, unconscious, 'soulless' mystical throbbing." Lewis looks behind the literary aspects of the writing to evaluate each writer's *Weltanschauung*, and to trace its genesis. He sees Walt Whitman as the "Father of the American Baby," responsible for the cult of the sensual: "Walt showed all those enthusiastic expansive habits that we associate with the Baby. He rolled about naked in the Atlantic surf, uttering 'barbaric yawps,' as he called them, in an ecstasy of primitive exhibitionism."

A month after the appearance of the second *Enemy*, Lewis was writing to Herbert Read asking for a contribution. It is essential, he writes, "not to give the impression of a single spy, but of a battalion." And when *The Criterion* looked like closing down, Lewis offered T. S. Eliot, the editor, and some of his staff, positions on *The Enemy*. This was not to be, and the third and final issue of *The Enemy* appeared in January 1929 with only two poems masquerading as Lewis's "battalion." The main article is "The Diabolical Principle": a counter-attack against the *transition* article "First Aid to The Enemy" which was written by the Paris magazine's editors, and printed in December 1927. Among other things, it accused Lewis of being a "good old Tory at heart," "about seven tenths bluff," xenophobic, and reactionary. They attack "The Enemy" with an anecdote worthy of Lewis himself:

Colonel Mouffetard had made a considerable fortune in one of the colonies before he had passed middle age and because, it was said, the laws were somewhat archaic and had remained several years behind his methods, had left Africa just about eight minutes ahead of the sheriff. His wife had been pious and jealous. He had been susceptible and vigorous. At the time of the story, he was still susceptible, and his wife was in a rather comfortable asylum. He had white hair, yellowed like old parchment, which he parted exactly in the middle, and he was so careful of his dress that his valet had to measure the length of his sleeves each morning with a tape.

After having had more than five hundred women, not counting the very blackest, he fell desperately in love with a beautiful young milliner in Troyes who had a good singing voice and wished to cultivate it. M. Mouffetard set her up in a magnificent apartment, hired the best teachers he could find, and spent his entire time in an amorous frenzy. As is often the case with an old man and a young girl, things went well.

At last, however, Suzanne was offered a part in a musical comedy in Paris and in spite of M. Mouffetard's tears, threats, loss of weight, or even convulsions, she decided that she could not forego a career. As the day approached for her to depart, and the horrid realization crystallized in M. Mouffetard's mind, he began to groan and to pray, staring at the hooks where her clothes, now in the trunk, had hung. The clockhands crept around, and finally the taxi called at the door. He clung to her and kissed her at the top of the stairs, but as she descended and walked down the path, so fresh and lovely, all other emotions were volatilized into a consuming fury and in speechless defiance of whatever gods he had, he rushed down the stairs and as she stepped into the auto, delivered her the most terrific and resounding kick in the behind which had ever echoed on that quiet street.

In reading Mr. Lewis' *The Enemy* we were reminded of old Colonel Mouffetard and his ambitious sweetheart, for it seems to us that instead of his leaving supposed revolutionary camps, as he would have it appear, modern literature has found a chance for something better and has left poor Wyndham dolefully behind. Consequently he takes a farewell boot at the rump he had fondled so coyly a few years before. We think literature will recover. (161–162)

In "The Diabolical Principle" Lewis aims his boot firmly at Jolas, Paul, and Sage, editors of *transition,* and all connected with that magazine. Their periodical represents everything that is wrong with the *Zeitgeist*: politically, morally, and aesthetically, "they exult in the romantic chaos around them and seek to intensify it." As in "Paleface," Lewis's criticism looks beyond literary values to lay bare the philosophical bases of their particular moral vision. His analysis of the *transition* attitude is doom-laden, seeing them—

communists to a man—as about to usher in a new age of Nihilism. Gertrude Stein who, with Joyce, was closely associated with *transition*, comes in for more criticism in this article:

> *Miss Gertrude Stein should get out of english.* That is quite the first step. If Stein got out of english she would get out of english more thoroughly than Joyce (who is half in and half out) and she would then duly lead that able Dublin executant into a manner where together they might concoct not a bad new tongue. (13)

The linguistic anarchy of Stein and Joyce is only part of the break-up of all accepted values in the contemporary cult of revolt, says Lewis. This particular aspect of the "politicization of art" is characterized by the motif of romantic, satanic revolt: the Surrealists (and, by implication, *transition*), in denying the reality of the "real," throw out all civilized values. This is one more aspect of the surrender to the flux, and was, for Lewis, a denial of life: for only by struggling against chaos could one create things of value.

"The Diabolical Principle" is too obviously full of animus to be regarded as anything other than a brilliant, virtuoso piece of "blasting" polemics. Yet this is one of the attractive features of Lewis's pamphleteering: it is a deeply involved defence, if not of his own writing, then of values he passionately espoused. Unlike the conventional periodical, Lewis's journals appeared when he felt something needed saying; they were literary hustings from which he held forth on his many and various disputes with the *Zeitgeist*. The proposed *Enemy* No. 4 never appeared, and nineteen years after the publication of the third issue, Lewis was still talking hopefully of restarting the venture, but, as he stressed in his first editorial "no guarantee can be given as to its punctual appearance."

Much of *The Enemy* was reprinted in book-form, and even during this prolific period, Lewis was rewriting many of his earlier publications. *Time and Western Man* and *The Childermass* brought limited critical acclaim, but it was with *The Apes of God* that Lewis was again subjected to the type of publicity which surrounded the *enfant bizarre* of the *Blast* days. Lewis was dissatisfied with the offer made by Chatto and Windus, and his own creation, *The Arthur Press*, published the satire. When Roy

Campbell's commissioned review of the novel was turned down by the *New Statesman*'s acting editor, Ellis Roberts, Lewis skilfully transformed the rejection into excellent publicity. *The Arthur Press* brought out "Enemy Pamphlet No. 1," entitled *The History of a Rejected Review*, which printed Campbell's piece and other laudatory comments. Lewis summed up the reaction to his novel in this way:

> *The Apes of God* appeared upon June 3rd last. Immediately an electrical atmosphere pervaded all the London District. In a hundred ways Mr. Wyndham Lewis was made to feel he had *gone too far*. Anonymous letters of the most violent sort have flowed in at the letter box. His life has even been threatened by an airman! The "Agony Column" of *The Times* has resounded with the distress of a certain person who imagined himself attacked in *The Apes of God*. A certain poetess, who supposed herself an "ape," had a seizure as she caught sight of Mr. Lewis's advancing sombrero in a Bayswater street, and had to be led into a chemist's shop.

The Apes of God marked the beginning of one of the most famous literary feuds of the day. The Sitwells had all sat for Lewis—indeed his portrait of Edith is one of his finest—but even in 1922, as she explained in a letter, relations were strained:

> I knew Lewis very well, because I sat to him every day excepting Sundays, for ten months. It was impossible to like him, and in the end his attitude became so threatening that I ceased to sit for him, so that the portrait of me by him in the Tate has no hands. . . . When one sat to him in his enormous studio, mice emerged from their holes, and lolled against the furniture, staring in the most insolent manner at the sitter. At last when Tom Eliot was sitting to him, their behaviour became intolerable. They climbed on to his knee, and would sit staring up at his face. So Lewis bought a large gong which he placed near the mouse-hole, and, when matters reached a certain limit, he would strike this loudly, and the mice would retreat. (*Selected Letters of Edith Sitwell*, 231)

Although not technically "Bloomsbury," Lewis seems to have regarded the Sitwells as part of that socio-aesthetic world. On his side, the public feud was waged in all awareness of its ridiculous nature. After *The Apes of God*, the Sitwells revenged themselves upon the reputedly paranoid Lewis by regularly sending anonymous letters and meaningless postcards from all ends of England and Europe. Edith writes to a friend:

> Once I pricked my big toe and planted the mark on the p.c. and wrote "Rache" on it. We also sent him raving mad telegrams. I got one sent to him from Calais to his address in Percy Street, which ran thus—(the German is a reference to his book on Hitler):
> Percy Wyndham Lewis, 21 Percy Street, etc. Achtung. Nicht hinauslehnen. Uniformed commissar man due. Stop. Better wireless help. Last night too late. Love. Ein Freund. Signed Lewis Wyndham, 21 Percy Street.
> And two days ago he got a telegram saying "Achtung. Nicht hinauslehnen. The Bear dances." Meanwhile Osbert's secretary lost one of her teeth, which snapped off, and Osbert sent it to Lewis with Sir Gerald du Maurier's card, which he happened to have. Also L. hates being thought to be a Jew, and Osbert's secretary, finding out that a man called Sieff is organizing an exhibition of Jewish artists, has written in the unfortunate Sieff's name to Lewis, asking him to exhibit, with the result that Lewis and Sieff are having a fearful row, and all the Jewish artists are vowing vengeance on Lewis for insulting their race. (*Ibid.*, 43–44)

These practical jokes of "God's own Peterpaniest family" must have sometimes worried Lewis who, from his earliest days, could be intensely suspicious of those he did not implicitly trust. But he seems generally to have taken all this in good part, for in *Blasting and Bombardiering* he can write of Edith: "She is one of my most hoary, tried and reliable enemies. We are two good old enemies, Edith and I, *inseparables* in fact. I do not think I should be exaggerating if I described myself as Miss Sitwell's *favourite enemy*. . . . The Sitwell family . . . are one of my comic turns." Apart from the transient ripostes of the Sitwells, Edith caricatured Lewis in her novel *I Live Under a Black Sun* (1937), but, compared to the ape-portraits of the Finnian-Shaws, the caricature of Lewis is far less of a literary insult. The Finnian-Shaws are transformed into hideous, sycophantic and moronic grotesques, with just enough information for the identification with the Sitwells to be made:

> In colour Lord Osmund was a pale coral, with flaxen hair brushed tightly back, his blond pencilled pap rising straight from his sloping forehead: galb-like wings to his nostrils—the goat-like profile of

Edward the Peacemaker. The lips were curved. They were thickly profiled as though belonging to a moslem portrait of a stark-lipped sultan. His eyes, vacillating and easily discomfited, slanted down to the heavy curved nose. Eyes, nose, and lips contributed to one effect, so that they seemed one feature. It was the effect of the jouissant animal—the licking, eating, sniffing, fat-muzzled machine— dedicated to Wine, Womanry, and Free Verse-cum-soda-water. (*The Apes of God*, 371)

In contrast, Edith Sitwell's portrait of Henry Debingham is much closer to what Lewis called a "dramatized social news-sheet" of the early Huxley brand. In terms of their literary badinage, the Swiftean intensity of Lewis completely outmatches the restrained rejoinder of Edith Sitwell.

After a long lay-off from painting during the twenties, Lewis began again in the thirties. He was troubled by a recurring illness and in order to keep the pot boiling and to pay for nursing homes he was forced to write more journalism than he wished. Lewis despaired of the state of art in the modern world: he saw the Dadaists reducing art to a joke and making a mockery of those artists who were attempting serious experimental work. "Unless something is done to preserve it, and to keep alive the few artists who are able to do it—life may flicker out. Our grandchildren may lisp: 'What *were* artists, mama? Why aren't there any now?' " Lewis learned at first hand from his exhibition at the Leicester Galleries in 1937 that the interest in the visual arts was no longer as vital as it once had been. He worked frantically at preparations for the show—one oil still being wet when it was hung—but of the twenty-four paintings in the exhibition, only one was sold during the first week. Geoffrey Grigson, a staunch supporter of Lewis, organized what was, in effect, a quasi-petition to *The Times*, signed by twenty influential personalities, saying that this was a slight to a great artist. As a result, the Tate Gallery purchased "Red Scene," the first painting bought by a public collection, and four others were sold privately, but this did not greatly alter Lewis's financial position:

> "A blood vessel will burst in my big toe," he wrote to a dealer, "if economic tension does not terminate. Returning home this afternoon, I found a wolf at the door, his teeth bared; next week is going to be awkward." (*Letters*, 238)

Lewis's reputation was at its nadir in the thirties. His *Hitler* (1931), which reprinted a series of articles he had written for *Time and Tide*, was taken as the key book of his *oeuvre*—the fruit of *The Art of Being Ruled*. In retrospect, one can see that Lewis—like some English politicians—misguidedly believed that Hitler was a rational man. In attacking Communism—always a Lewisian bogey—Hitler was accepted by Lewis as "A Man of Peace":

> I do not think that if Hitler had his way he would bring the fire and the sword across otherwise peaceful frontiers. He would, I am positive, remain peacefully at home, fully occupied with the internal problems of the *Dritte Reich*. And, as regards, again, the vexed question of the "antisemitic" policy of his party, in that I believe Hitler himself—once he had obtained power—would show increasing moderation and tolerance. (47–48)

As an over-reaction against the threat of Communism, *Hitler* shares many similarities with another collection of hasty journalism, *Left Wings Over Europe* (1936). Lewis subtitled this latter book *How to Make a War About Nothing* and it is, in part, an *apologia* for German foreign policy. Even if there were a war, writes Lewis, "the marxist interests would never allow it to stop . . . until it had made a sahara of the world." Lewis, of course, realized only too well his differences with the prevailing consensus of political opinion among the intelligentsia, yet never attempted to compromise his beliefs: "My political book (*Left Wings*) is rather markedly anti-Left-wing," he wrote to Father D'Arcy, "and I do not know what the good old Liberal publisher who is at present examining it will decide." Such attitudes brought about what Roy Campbell has described as a "Lewis boycott." This was a time, wrote the right-wing Campbell, "when one's bread and butter depended on thinking pro-Red," and although "not an actual branch of the Civil Service, the Book Trade in England with its ramifications in the Press, is very much like one of the Ministries, say, of Food or Labour, and the authors and reviewers can be compared to the officials, administrative clerks, and chairborne stamplickers, who issue forms for literary success or failure according as one keeps to the rules and regulations. To generate ideas of one's own was a criminal offence. . . ." Of the three novels after *The Apes of God*—*Snooty Baronet* (1932), *The*

Revenge for Love (1937) and *The Vulgar Streak* (1941)—none sold more than 3,000 copies, and as early as *One-Way Song* (1933), Lewis was wryly versifying on his position as "*poeto maladetto*":

> I am even excluded too
> From all official mention—all except *Who's Who*.
> I am an outcast and a man "maudit."
> But how romantic! Don't you envy me?
> A sort of Villon, bar the gallows: but
> Even there I may be accommodated yet.
> Why yes it's very jolly to be picked
> As the person not so much to be kicked,
> As the person who de facto *is not there*,
> As the person relegated to the dark back-stair.
> "Outcast" is good, in a system of shark and gull,
> Where all that's "illustrious" is also untouchable!
> A solitary honour. To be he
> For whose benefit *unmentionability*
> Has been invented, as a new order of the Dead
> Who yet exist.

Lewis collected some of his literary journalism for his major critical work of the thirties, *Men Without Art* (1934). Worried about the book's reception, he wrote asking a friend "What is the opinion of the Town . . . about my Artless Men? Any hard feelings?" Similarly, he wrote to Herbert Read (from the characteristically secretive "Pall Mall Safe Deposit" address) enquiring if he, Read, had written the unsympathetic left-wing review in *The Times Literary Supplement*. Lewis's lack of popular success, of course, is not to be considered solely due to a political boycott; there are other, very obvious, reasons why he was not a popular writer. In the introduction to *Men Without Art* he states the basic position for any reader of his work. It is not, to say the least, a working-philosophy calculated to gain a mass-audience: "you must be prepared to work a little bit, to look an abstract idea in the face and mildly cudgel your brains." This was obviously too much to ask of a wide readership—but, even in the thirties, Lewis had a not inconsiderable following. Surprisingly enough, many of them were extremely left-wing. When the double number of *Twentieth Century Verse* (November/December 1937) was devoted to Lewis, he wrote to the editor, Julian Symons: "I am a little abashed. No company, this, for a public enemy. I am very much afraid that you have compromised me! I have perused these articles rather in the way a notorious bandit would a shower of *many-happy-returns* and other obliging messages, at his birthday breakfast table in his hideout, from the local constabulary."

Lewis had no need to worry about the "local constabulary" losing their nerve. The portrait of T. S. Eliot submitted to the Royal Academy for the 1938 exhibition was rejected by the Hanging Committee, and there then followed yet another bitter, very public, row. Augustus John resigned from the Royal Academy in protest; a broadcast speech by Winston Churchill at the R.A. banquet kept alive the controversy. Churchill had sided with the Academy's "authority and respect for authority," and Lewis replied to this "passionate advocacy of platitude" in *The Times*. But publicity alone does not pay bills, and even another exhibition of his paintings in June–July 1938 did not ease financial problems. Finding the "pursuit of his profession none too easy," Lewis was attracted by an offer of work in America and in August 1939 the Lewises set sail for what was intended to be a short working-holiday.

Before the Lewises reached America, war had been declared, and they "zig-zagged across" the Atlantic "with life-belts on." Eventually sold to the Durban Municipal Art Gallery, the "rejected portrait" brought in enough money to finance the early days of their stay in America. Through a contact at Buffalo University, Lewis received a commission to paint the portrait of the Chancellor, for which he was paid "500 bucks after the minimum of parley." But hopes of further commissions did not materialize in Buffalo, and for the next year Lewis lived in New York, picking up portrait commissions wherever possible. In reality, America was no more congenial to the artist than the England Lewis had left; to make matters worse, his name did not carry as much weight on that side of the Atlantic:

> My efforts to obtain journalistic work have been equally unsuccessful. During twelve months spent in or near New York, it has been impossible to make any arrangement with a gallery, or to sell a scratch or a smudge of any kind. (*Letters*, 276)

41

Without friends, money, or prospects, and in the knowledge that their visa was not renewable, they "scuttled," rather unceremoniously, into Canada in November 1940.

The change of surroundings gave Lewis hope; the Canadians at first seemed more aware of English culture than the Americans had been, and Toronto was promising: "After the winter of my discontent in the long and chilly shadow of the Statue of Liberty, I feel as if I had come up out of a coal-mine or a dungeon into the fresh air again." Within a month of arriving, Lewis was giving radio talks, lecturing, and had promises of portrait commissions; but it was difficult to find publishers for his writing, and it was not always easy to get money into Canada from England. Toronto soon palled: "I feel that someone is sitting on my chest—having, to start with, gagged me—and singing Moody and Sankey all day long . . . I have been living up in this sanctimonious ice-box . . . painting portraits of the opulent Methodists of Toronto." Lewis turned these hellish experiences into *Self Condemned* (1954), one of his finest novels. When commissions began to falter, Lewis feared that he could "end his days in a Toronto flop-house"; on top of all else, his optician diagnosed glaucoma and possibly blindness within six months. It was with a desperate, wry humour that Lewis wrote to a friend: ". . . if my eyes go I go too. Loathsome as the world is, I do like to *see* it. That sort of blackout I could not live in."

From the depths of this despair in the Hotel Tudor, Toronto, Lewis produced some of the most beautiful water-colours of his career. He longed for a secure position—such as resident artist at a university—but was forced to go on painting portraits and "struggling with people about the shapes of their noses and the size of their feet." The diagnosis of impending blindness did eventually prove correct, but Lewis was spared another decade of sight before he was "pushed into an unlighted room, the door banged and locked forever." He scraped together enough commissions to exist for two years in Toronto, but his letters during this time are full of scarcely disguised pleas for help. In February 1943, when offered a lectureship at Assumption College, Windsor, Ontario, he was delighted at the prospect of economic security. Lewis took classes on philosophy and literature, and even though the intellectual *ethos* of Windsor was much more congenial, he still longed to return to England. A letter from Augustus John reminded him that there was, "however inaccessible, a more civilized and intelligent world" than the one in which he had existed for six years. In August 1945 the Lewises were back at their bomb-damaged flat in London.

Almost immediately, Lewis began regularly reviewing for *The Listener*, and he remained their art critic until forced to retire through impending blindness in 1951. Lewis felt that culturally, everything was "drying up" in England. Extremism was eating away at the arts and "the rot" had set into contemporary life at all levels; his letters are full of complaints about the discomforts and inconveniences of post-war England: "What I always fear about this country is that I shall be asked to dispense with glass at my windows." A lot of time was taken up in achieving the basic comforts of life, and his annoyance with everyday trivia is, in turn, comic and pathetic: the stove in his studio "wastes about $2\frac{1}{2}$ hours out of the twenty-four"; English bread makes him constipated; the house has dry rot ("pursued by a mad carpenter"); the jam is adulterated with turnip; the water is almost undrinkable —"When the taste of the chlorine wears off, you taste the sewage, which is worse. . . . This is the capital of a dying empire—not crashing down in flames and smoke but expiring in a peculiar muffled way." This was the England Lewis portrayed in his book of short stories entitled *Rotting Hill* (1951)—Pound's name for Notting Hill, where the Lewises lived—and in his final novel *The Red Priest* (1956). "Wyndham Lewis" is the protagonist of some of the "nonfiction stories" of *Rotting Hill* which reveal the paralysis at the heart of post-war London as surely as did Joyce's *Dubliners* of that eponymous city. These stories are remarkably evocative of post-war England, and, as quasi-fictional reportage, they reveal a vigorous mind challenging a depressed and depressing era.

Having lost touch with Ezra Pound, Lewis was amazed by his "incomprehensible intervention in World War II (when in some moment of poetic frenzy he mistook the clownish Duce for Thomas Jefferson)." It saddened him to think of his old friend incarcerated in St. Elizabeth's, and he threw himself into the campaign for Pound's release—even suggesting to T. S. Eliot that they should organize a petition themselves. For ten years Lewis kept in touch with the Pounds; his early bantering letters attempted to make light of the situation: "I am told that you believe yourself to be Napoleon—or is it Mussolini? What a pity you didn't choose Buddha while you were about it, instead of a politician." But as the years went on, the valedictory "Best wishes for freedom in New Year," sounded less and less hopeful. It became evident that agitation from outside America was not helping Pound, who, furthermore, was not at all tractable to suggestions as to how best secure a free pardon. It was a somewhat frustrated T. S. Eliot who wrote to Lewis: "Possibly it would be a good thing to get him out even if the way he was got out didn't please him." Lewis kept in touch with Pound until the end of his life, and a letter written in Lewis's last months shows him still solicitous for Pound's welfare.

Some of the material from Lewis's notes and lectures in America went into *America and Cosmic Man* (1948), which defined the "new species of man" being produced by the cultural "melting pot" of the United States; many of these notions about the "advance-copy of a future world order" look forward to McLuhan's "global village" world-view. Lewis welcomed the "thunderous murmurs of a cradle song"—Cosmic Man is in his infancy:

> In the region of ideas, the "melting-pot" is in full operation. Further, the traditions and beliefs inhering in these so-called "regions" are subject to dissipation and decay, and what is very much to the point, no new "regions" will take the place of those now moribund. We shall have a full fledged universal culture before we have a universal society, unfortunately. (159)

Celebrating the rise of "cosmopolitanism," this book reverses many of Lewis's attacks on centralization which he called in *Left Wings* "the greatest evil it is possible to imagine." Lewis's last work of socio-aesthetics, *The Demon of Progress in the Arts* (1954), carries on the defence of art in the face of a rampant, fashionable extremism in which "only zero is tolerated": "one is moved to curse these impostors for the death of art which they are attempting to achieve." Herbert Read, "Mister Abreast-of-the-Times," personifies the urge to novelty: "he is the writer who has led the Salvation Army into a Promised Land, into an Institute. And, if you will tolerate more imagery of this kind, he has done

his best to lure Mammon into this tabernacle." Looking back to
his Vorticist days, Lewis saw that the first occurrence of this
aesthetic "foot and mouth" was in himself. Another scourge—the
war—drove out the first: "I saw that it was irrational to attempt
to transmute the art of painting into music—to substitute for the
most naturally concrete of arts the most inevitably abstract. So of
course I recovered my reason. . . . For what I was headed for,
obviously, was to fly away from the world of men, of pigs, of
chickens, of alligators, and to live on the unwatered moon, only
a moon sawed up into square blocks, in the most alarming way.
What an escape I had!" (3)

Lewis was very successful as *The Listener*'s art critic, and started
one or two "Enemy" controversies with his outspoken judgments,
yet he also gave much encouragement to young painters. His large
retrospective exhibition in May 1949 was financially rewarding,
and he achieved some measure of public recognition when, in
1951, he was granted a small civil list pension, and, the following
year, awarded the honorary degree of D.Litt by Leeds University.
He was conscious of the literary *persona* his writings portrayed,
and pointed out the "discrepancy between Mr. W. L. the writer
and my own easy-going, anything but contentious self." Yet the
defiant streak of the old campaigner never deserted him, and when
the London County Council were about to pull down their Notting
Hill flat, Lewis suggested (in a *Daily Mail* interview) that Colonel
Nasser was just the man to help him deal with the L.C.C.
demolition squad. Accepting blindness philosophically, Lewis was
aware of the irony inherent in the situation: that one who set so
much store by the visual should be deprived of sight: "But it is
after all the kind of thing one has to expect if one allows oneself
to be born. Had I been a suitably obstreperous foetus all this
could have been avoided."

In 1954 *Self Condemned* was published and many critics
thought it Lewis's finest novel: Ezra Pound wrote affirming that it
"Shd git yu the Nobble." Its success was followed by the broadcast
of *The Human Age* on the BBC Third Programme in May 1955,
which was called by Walter Allen a "great occasion in broad-
casting and contemporary writing." In 1951, D. G. Bridson's
dramatized version of Lewis's *The Childermass* had been broadcast,
and because of public reaction, the Third Programme commis-

sioned Lewis to finish *The Human Age*. It was an act of great foresight on the part of Bridson, and great generosity on behalf of the BBC; Lewis was given two years of economic security in which to complete the work. This freedom gave him the impetus to create, and even though very ill, he was full of enthusiasm. Totally blind, Lewis would write in longhand, measuring with his fingers the distance between the lines. His wife would then read back to him the almost illegible script, making alterations suggested by Lewis, before typing the work. Often a wandering line in the manuscript reveals a lapse into unconsciousness brought on by the brain tumour which was finally to cause his death. The agreement with the BBC was that Lewis should write the two sequels in novel form, and they would then be dramatized by Bridson for radio production. The novels which resulted from this agreement confirmed T. S. Eliot's "suspicion" that Lewis was "the most distinguished living novelist" of the day.

The highlight of Lewis's last years was undoubtedly the Tate Gallery's exhibition "Wyndham Lewis and Vorticism" (July 1956), which, although seriously ill, he managed to attend. It was the largest showing of Lewis's own work, and also collected paintings of other Vorticists; but even this final moment of recognition was not free of controversy. Angered by the dominance of Lewis's work in the exhibition (he was represented by 159 out of 197 catalogued exhibits), William Roberts privately published a highly critical pamphlet entitled "The Resurrection of Vorticism and the Apotheosis of Wyndham Lewis." Lewis, of course, was incensed by the attack, but "The Enemy" was too ill to counter, and the row was left to others in the correspondence columns of the *Times Literary Supplement*. Lewis died in hospital on March 7, 1957. "A great intellect has gone," wrote Eliot in *The Sunday Times* obituary, "a great modern writer is dead."

2

Natures, Puppets and Wars

Looking back on his first published writings, Lewis recalled their genesis in his "long vague periods of indolence" in Brittany:

> The Atlantic air, the raw rich visual food of the barbaric environment, the squealing of the pipes, the crashing of the ocean, induced a creative torpor. Mine was now a drowsy sun-baked ferment, watching with delight the great comic effigies which erupted beneath my rather saturnine but astonished gaze.... The characters I chose to celebrate—Bestre, the Cornac and his wife, Brotcotnaz, le père François—were all primitive creatures, immersed in life, as much as birds, or big, obsessed, sun-drunk insects. (*Rude Assignment*, 117)

These primitive creatures were eventually to emerge as "wild bodies" in the 1927 collection of that name, but in their early form these pieces are not, in the accepted sense of the term, short stories. They are plotless travel sketches peopled by Breton "characters" whose idiosyncratic social relationships are the *raison d'être* of the vignettes.

"The Pole" was published in Hueffer's *The English Review* in May 1909; it was, Lewis recalled, "my first success of a practical nature." An exercise in imaginative social psychology, "The Pole" describes the curious phenomenon of permanent Slav boarders at Breton *pensions*. With the analytical eye of the social scientist, Lewis states his proposition at the outset; the remainder of the piece offers illustrative case-histories and inductive generalizations about the type. These early stories, wrote Lewis twenty-five years later, were "the crystallization of what I had to keep out of my consciousness while painting," and although the eye of the *visuel* is very obvious, it is usually subordinate to the polemical design of the whole.

"Some Innkeepers and Bestre," Lewis's second publication, appeared in the following issue of *The English Review* and showed similar preoccupations.

> The truest type of innkeeper is to be found in France. And as these papers deal with some of my experiences in Brittany last summer it is chiefly with France that I am concerned. (473)

"These papers" suggests that Lewis saw his early publications as imaginative reportage or documentaries rather than fictions, and his tone is often that of the sociologist—of the recorder rather than the creator:

> So the study of the French innkeeper is especially fruitful, for he veritably puts his whole soul into his part, everything in him blossoms prodigiously within the conventional limits of his trade. (479)

The reality that Lewis records, however, is not at all mundane. Delighting in the absurd, the grotesque and the bizarre, the more civilized "I" of the narrative wanders amongst the primitive "sun-drunk insects" assiduously noting their behavioural tics and exploring the tensions between roles and personalities. "So subtle is their method and manner of charming the public that it has an opposite effect," writes Lewis of his "eccentric exponents" of the astonishing art of innkeeping. As if to support his general truth by concrete evidence, Lewis appends—as *exemplum* to *moralitas* —the case-history of Bestre.

In *The English Review* version of the story, rather than seeing Bestre in action, the reader is told *about* his furious and demonic battles of glares. Presentation of character is limited by the exemplary role in which it functions—like the Poles, Bestre is a footnote in Lewis's thesis in social psychology. When these stories were reworked for publication in *The Wild Body* (1927) it was, however, the sociological aspect which was relegated to the foot-notes, and the characters, rather than the thesis, become the *raison d'être* of the writing. In turning "The Pole" into "Beau Séjour," Lewis is not so insistent in his attempts to "nail things down"; the discursive exposition becomes a short story and, in

Lawrence's phrase, the characters "get up and walk away with the nail." From the multiplicity of minor characters in "The Pole," Lewis selects the *ménage* of Mme Peronette, Carl and Zoborov, placing their interrelationship into a formal framework. Picaresque meanderings take on beginning, middle and end; minor characters, if not omitted altogether, are strictly subordinated to the central relationship. Similarly, in the transition from "Some Innkeepers and Bestre" to "Bestre" (as it appears in *The Wild Body*), the prolegomenous, discursive material—"Some Innkeepers"—is filtered out completely, leaving the magnificently grotesque Bestre at the centre of the stage.

Although *The Wild Body* is still very much written to a thesis, this is not expressed in exegetical running commentaries as in the early versions, but stated separately in two essays, "Inferior Religions" and "The Meaning of the Wild Body." These expound the philosophical assumptions which underlie the comic vision of the stories:

> First, to assume the dichotomy of mind and body is necessary here, without arguing it; for it is upon that essential separation that the theory of laughter here proposed is based . . . we have to postulate *two* creatures, one that never enters into life, but that travels about in a vessel to whose destiny it is momentarily attached. That is, of course, the laughing observer, and the other is the Wild Body. . . . There is nothing that is animal (and we as bodies are animals) that is not absurd. This sense of the absurdity, or, if you like, the madness of our life, is at the root of every true philosophy. (243–244)

Reason is the "laughing observer" and the "wild body" is the autonomic physiological system to which it is fettered. Not only can the reflective intellect observe the absurdities of others, but— standing back from the wild body in which it is housed—it can apprehend its own absurdity. In the light of this Cartesian dualism, there is something fundamentally absurd in the very fact of human existence; Kerr-Orr, the narrator, recognizes this in himself as well as in others:

> This forked, strange-scented, blond-skinned gut-bag, with its two bright rolling marbles with which it sees, bull's-eyes full of mockery

and madness, is my stalking-horse. I hang somewhere in its midst operating it with detachment. (5)

It is Kerr-Orr's Socratic awareness of his own position which places him above the mechanistic wild bodies. He operates his autonomic system: the wild bodies are operated by theirs. Representing mind over matter, he struts through the Breton countryside searching out bizarre examples of the machine in control of the operator or "the thing" running away with "the person."

Lewis's concept of comedy, of course, derives a great deal from Bergson and, as Geoffrey Wagner has written, "Bergson's *Le Rire* is a primer of Lewisian Satire." The French philosopher's basic point about comedy—that it is "la transformation d'une personne en chose"—becomes the crux of Lewis's definition:

> The root of the Comic is to be sought in the sensations resulting from the observations of a *thing* behaving like a person. But from that point of view all men are necessarily comic: for they are all *things*, or physical bodies, behaving as *persons*. . . . To bring vividly to our mind what we mean by "absurd," let us turn to the plant, and enquire how the plant could be absurd. Suppose you came upon an orchid or a cabbage reading Flaubert's *Salambo*, or Plutarch's *Moralia*, you would be very much surprised. But if you found a man or woman reading it, you would *not* be surprised.
>
> Now in one sense you ought to be just as much surprised at finding a man occupied in this way as if you had found an orchid or a cabbage, or a tom-cat, to include the animal world. There is the same physical anomaly. It is just as absurd externally, that is what I mean.—The deepest root of the Comic is to be sought in this anomaly. (246–247)

Paraded and presented by Kerr-Orr, *The Wild Body* is a collection of such anomalies.

Kerr-Orr is the Lewis-man of these stories, and the *persona* is representative of a type which recurs throughout Lewis's fiction—"the nature." In *The Art of Being Ruled* (1926), Goethe's distinction between puppets and natures is quoted with approbation. *Homo stultus* is mechanical, puppet-like, ignorant: "Natures," the super-species, are distinguished by self-awareness and control. Even if all men *are* fundamentally absurd, some are less so than others—Kerr-Orr is one of these:

I know much more about myself than people generally do. For instance I am aware that I am a barbarian. By rights I should be paddling about in a coracle. My body is large, white and savage. But all the fierceness has become transformed into *laughter*. . . . Everywhere where formerly I would fly at throats, I now howl with laughter. . . . My sense of humour in its mature phase has arisen in this very acute consciousness of what is *me*. In playing that off against another hostile *me*, that does not like the smell of mine, probably finds my large teeth, height and so forth abominable, I am in a sense working off my alarm at myself. So I move on a more primitive level than most men, I expose my essential *me* quite coolly, and all men shy a little. . . . I will show you myself in action, manoeuvring in the heart of reality. (3–4, 5, 7)

This physically primitive "soldier of humour" has harnessed his natural violence. As his mind gazes dispassionately upon his own "anomalies" and upon the world's, the fundamental ubiquitous absurdity gives rise to a philosophy of laughter:

It sprawls into everything. It has become my life. The result is that I am *never* serious about anything. I simply cannot help converting everything into burlesque patterns. (4)

It is as a connoisseur of the grotesque that Kerr-Orr catalogues specimens for his human menagerie. Anxious to catch the slightest comic nuances of behaviour, he installs himself in the midst of his exhibits, often acting as catalyst as well as recorder:

It was almost as though Fabre could have established himself within the masonries of the bee, and lived on its honey, while investigating for the human species. (120)

The physical closeness of Kerr-Orr's scrutiny—like a gorgonian lens—turns people into things. The description of Ludo, the blind Breton beggar, petrifies the living face into a mask—physiognomy becomes form.

As I looked at him I realized how the eyes mount guard over the face, as well as look out of it. The faces of the blind are hung there like a dead lantern. Blind people must feel on their skins our eyes upon them: but this sheet of flesh is rashly stuck up in what must appear far outside their control, an object in a foreign world of sight. So in consequence of this divorce, their faces have the appearance of things that have been abandoned by the mind. What

51

is his face to a blind man? Probably nothing more than an organ, an exposed part of the stomach, that is a mouth. (179)

This is what Lewis elsewhere calls "the truth of Natural Science" as opposed to the "truth of Romance": the non-human gaze which plays over the "dry shells and pelts of things," confining itself to the "visible machinery of life" ("Studies in the Art of Laughter").

While action explodes all around, Kerr-Orr, like a ringmaster in a well-organized arena, surveys and controls his charges with consummate ease. He is "the showman to whom the antics and solemn gambols of these wild children are to be a source of strange delight" (232). This is not the Lawrentian fascination with the primitive: Lewis is less interested in the differences between the civilized and the unsophisticated, and more in their similarities. The Breton peasants exhibit, writ large, the "solemn gambols" of all humanity. In laughing at them we are not, like visitors to Elizabethan asylums, laughing at these "carefully selected specimens of religious fanaticism" (234). These grotesques are not on show as curious mutations of nature. Lewis postulates no norm against which his madmen are to be measured, but rather suggests that this "madness" be taken into account in any definition of humanity. Driven by various permutations of *idées fixes*, ruling passions, fetishes and the arbitrary functioning of their autonomic systems, the wild bodies are units in "a new human mathematic," the basic premise of which is that "we have in most lives the spectacle of a pattern as circumscribed and complete as a theorem of Euclid" (233).

One such theorem is the ritual of violence performed by Brotcotnaz on his wife. These beatings are his bloody obeisance to dark gods. Julie, the wife, suffers her perpetual crucifixion in doleful silence:

> Her eyes are black and moist, with the furtive intensity of a rat. They move circumspectly in this bloated shell. She displaces herself also more noiselessly than the carefullest nun, and her hands are generally decussated, drooping upon the ridge of her waist-line, as though fixed there with an emblematic nail, at about the level of the navel. Her stomach is, for her, a kind of exclusive personal "calvary." At its crest hang her two hands, with the orthodox decussation, an elaborate ten-fingered symbol. (208)

The imagery suggests Julie's martyrdom at the hands of Brotcot-naz's "inferior religion": only the rat-like furtiveness of her eyes distances her from the conventional hagiological type. Julie, too, bows the knee to an inferior religion of her own: she secretly drinks, and attempts to pass off her bruises as "erysipelas." Although both "secrets" are widely known to friends and neighbours, Julie pretends, for form's sake, that certain things are true. The neighbours, also for form's sake, are party to the ground-rules of their private ritual and the whole affair becomes a complex skein of unspoken assumptions and understanding.

The Brotcotnazs' ceremony of violence is like the formal, highly-patterned dance they perform for Kerr-Orr. The steps are pre-ordained and there is no margin for improvisation. Yet there is no real contact: each partner is aware of what is to come, and the pattern exists independently of themselves:

> "Viens donc, Julie! Come then. Let us dance."
> Julie sat and sneered through her vinous mask at her fascinating husband. He insisted, standing over her with one toe pointed outward in the first movement of the dance, his hand held for her to take in a courtly attitude.
> "Viens donc, Julie! Dansons un peu!"
> Shedding shamefaced, pinched, and snuffling grins to right and left as she allowed herself to be drawn into this event, she rose. They danced a sort of minuet for me, advancing and retreating, curtseying and posturing, shuffling rapidly their feet. Julie did her part, it seemed, with understanding. (218)

The dance is a pastiche of reality; attitudes are donned like masks as these two peasants act out a courtly minuet. Just as the minuet exists beyond the dancers, or a Euclidean theorem beyond the page, so the violence of Brotcotnaz is almost impersonal, having its genesis beyond the personalities involved. Running in behavioural grooves seemingly too deeply scored to be changed, their life-style is as mindless a ritual of stimulus-response as that of Pavlovian salivating dogs. However, a near-fatal accident to Julie serves to break the pattern and, like an interrupted dance, things are never the same afterwards. The iconographical fetish of action is smashed, the "inferior religion" falls apart, and Brotcotnaz cannot assimilate the new events into his old ways.

The machinery of habit, the "religious" fascination of people for things, and people for people, all are functions of the wild body. The violent energy which erupts periodically in the brutality of Brotcotnaz is often a feature of these characters—in "The Cornac and His Wife" the violence is just as great, but exists beneath the surface, emerging as the performer's hatred of his audience. The Cornac is head of a troupe of itinerant acrobats who scrape a meagre living by giving displays to groups of Breton villagers. He and his wife have an "implacable grudge" against the spectators:

> With the man, obsessed by ill-health, the grievance against fortune was associated with the more brutal hatred that almost choked him every time he appeared professionally. . . . These displays involved the insane contortions of an indignant man and his dirty, breathless wife, of whose ugly misery it was required that a daily mournful exhibition should be made of her shrivelled legs, in pantomime hose. She must crucify herself with a scarecrow abandon, this iron and blood automaton, and affect to represent the factor of sex in a geometrical posturing. (136, 137–8)

As with Julie, this life is a self-willed perpetual crucifixion: habit is both torture and palliative; there is no escape from the ritual pattern of existence. The performance witnessed by Kerr-Orr is a ceremonial defiance of the audience. Because a local by-law forbids the appearance of his young daughter, the old man is forced to drag his own weary body through the painful contortions of the act for the pleasure of the audience. A "whistling sneer of hatred" acknowledges the applause; he is aware that they have come to see "the entire family break their necks one after the other" (139). The laughter of the clown and the crowd is another expression of this violence; another primitive response to the latent dangers of the act. "The herd-bellow at the circus is always associated with mock-violent events, however, and (this) true laughter is torn out of a tragic material" (162). The reflex actions that Lewis explores—the nervous laughter in the face of tragedy, the "brutal *frisson*" inspired by danger—are the gut-reactions and mysterious spasms of the human mechanism. As in a Giacometti sculpture, the "civilized" accretions which have gathered around the wild body are pared away, until, in these Breton peasants, "that small, primitive, literally antediluvian vessel in which we set out on our adventures" stands revealed.

Bestre, the finest creation of *The Wild Body*, is, like the Bailiff in *Childermass*, a superb grotesque. The story is very simple: Bestre, a Breton innkeeper, indulges in furious battles of glares with a Parisian artist and his wife. The plot charts the battle and details Bestre's tactics. Kerr-Orr is not interested in the depth-psychology of Bestre's obsession—the ruling passion is a *donnée*, its cause buried in the viscera or the subconscious—but he observes Bestre with such precision that his own activity borders on the obsessive. The prose is thick and glutinous—what Hugh Kenner has called "a species of verbal impasto"—full of biological imagery and verbs of startling action. Bestre emerges:

> His tongue stuck out, his lips eructated with the incredible indecorum that appears to be the monopoly of liquids, his brown arms were for the moment genitals, snakes in one massive twist beneath his mamillary slabs, gently riding on a pancreatic swell, each hair on his oil-bearing skin contributing its message of porcine affront. . . . On reaching the door into which he had sunk, plump and slick as into a stage trap, there he was inside—this grease-bred old mammifier—his tufted vertex charging about the plank ceiling— generally ricochetting like a dripping sturgeon in a boat's bottom —arms warm brown, ju-jitsu of his guts, tan canvas shoes and trousers rippling in ribbed planes as he darted about—with a filthy snicker for the scuttling female, and a stark cock of the eye for an unknown figure miles to his right: he filled this short tunnel with clever parabolas and vortices, little neat stutterings of triumph, goggle-eyed hypnotisms, in retrospect, for his hearers. (117–118)

Bestre is not exhibited, like the fat lady in the fair-ground booth, to be mocked as a freak. He is, in a sense, the hidden side of Everyman: if humanity, by definition, is all that humanity has produced, then Lewis, in these stories, is holding up the wild bodies as a mirror to the reader. Bestre's routines are as rigid as those of the donkey turning the water wheel, and his inferior religion is typical of the driving forces behind other *Wild Body* characters: Valmore's *idée fixe* that he is all-American dominates his life ("A Soldier of Humour"); Ludo, the blind beggar in "The Death of the Ankou," is hounded by a primitive death-god; Françoise has moulded his personality on the "emotions provoked by the bad, late, topical sentimental songs of Republican France" ("Franciscan Adventures"). All are automata: wound up by predilections, they whirr on their giddy way. The right response, according to Kerr-Orr, is a "bark of delight" at the proximity of such absurdities. Yet even in the recognition and enjoyment of the "stylistic anomalies," Kerr-Orr is himself absurd:

> Flinging myself on the bed, my blond poll rolling about in ecstasy upon the pillow, I howled like an exultant wolf. (29)

Observer and observed alike are implicated in the pervasive comic vision. For Lewis, any definition of human life must include this element of the absurd and in his description of "perfect laughter" ("Studies in the Art of Laughter"), he outlines this vision:

> *Perfect laughter* . . . would select as the objects of its mirth as much the antics dependent upon pathologic maladjustments, injury or disease, as the antics of clumsy and imperfectly functioning healthy people. . . . There is no reason at all why we should not burst out laughing at a foetus, for instance. We should after all, only be laughing *at ourselves!*—at ourselves early in our mortal career. (514)

In *Blasting and Bombardiering*, Lewis praised T. E. Hulme for "rubbing everybody's nose . . . in the highly disobliging doctrine" of Original Sin. There are many similarities between Hulme's *Weltanschauung* and Lewis's, and the former's dictum that "Man is in no sense perfect, but a wretched creature who can yet apprehend perfection" (*Speculations*), could well be taken as a definition of the *ethos* underlying much of Lewis's work. An aesthetic which sees satire as a universal "let-down" of the species and a technique of "human defamation" is akin, in many ways, to a notion of Original Sin—a secular Original Sin. This moral vision—implicit in *The Wild Body* and embodied more fully in *The Apes of God*—is voiced discursively in *The Art of Being Ruled*:

> Prostration is our natural position. A worm-like movement from a spot of sunlight to a spot of shade, and back, is the type of movement that is natural to men. As active, erect, and humane creatures they are in a constantly false position, and behaving in

an abnormal way. They have to be pushed up into it, and held there, till it has become a habit only to lie down at night; and at the first real opportunity they collapse and are full length once more. (281)

The vision is as profoundly despairing as that embodied in Swift's Struldbruggs or Beckett's Unnamable and *How It Is*. In the light of this philosophy, the wild bodies are representative of the yahoo in all humanity—yet something saves them from the total bleakness of, say, Lady Fredigonde in *The Apes of God*. Lewis, as well as Kerr-Orr, delights in—indeed "celebrates"—their absurdity. The satirical attitude here is ambiguous—as if Swift had, paradoxically, admired the vitality of his yahoos—and it is this very ambiguity which gives rise to the unique tone of *The Wild Body*. This is the stage prior to *The Apes of God*-attitude where human life is portrayed as "a very bad business indeed": here, it is very absurd indeed, and the artist revels in this absurdity.

Traces of the wild body *ethos* are to be found in a good deal of Lewis's writing outside *The Wild Body* itself. The early story "Unlucky for Pringle" which appeared in Douglas Goldring's magazine *The Tramp* (February, 1911), is very much part of this universe, but set in London instead of Brittany. James Pringle is a Kerr-Orr figure with a "gusto for the common circumstances of his life" and an aesthetic appreciation of rooms and their inhabit-ants as microcosms of an infinitely entertaining reality. Pringle's fastidiousness about the adequacy of rooms as studios has become removed from the realm of necessity to that of fascination. He changes rooms promiscuously, and "Rooms to Let" has a strange, sexual significance for him:

On the very frequently recurring occasions on which he set out to look for rooms he would savour the particular domestic taste of each new household he entered in the course of his search with the interest of a gourmet. Smiling strangely, as she thought, at the landlady who answered the door, he would at once go to her parlour—come for a debauch that she would never suspect. . . . He had passed like a ghost, in one sense, through a hundred unruffled households. Scores of peaceful landladies, like beautiful women caressed in their sleep by a spirit, had been enjoyed by him. Their drab apartments had served better than any boudoir. (404, 413)

Pringle rents a room from a French couple, the Chalarans, and installs himself in the midst of their life "like a worm in a wall," gradually usurping the indolent, wild-bodied Chalaran as patriarch. Sensing that he is being "enjoyed" by Pringle, Chalaran—in a series of marvellously indirect acts of cognitive dissonance— manages to oust this connoisseur of the ordinary. Chalaran, as much as Bestre or Brotcotnaz, is a wild body, whose frenetic and tangential outbursts are a *locus classicus* of deviations of object and aim:

> . . . in a burst of energy that lasted two afternoons (Chalaran) built a summer-house at the bottom of the garden. The summer-house, no doubt, saved Pringle. But had Pringle grasped then the at once compact and elemental character of these bursts of activity, and his own position as regards Chalaran, he would have shaken in his shoes. For who could say whether the next time a storm of such violence as to build a summer-house might not seize on some more substantial and apposite object. (413)

Similarly, the protagonist of "Sigismund" (a short story first published in 1920 and appended to *The Wild Body* collection in 1927) is an idiot son of an idiot tradition who, forever peering into the depths of his aristocratic past with pathological single-mindedness, is a wild body driven by a wild mind. Unlike the corporeal fixation of, say, Brotcotnaz for his wife—which is as physical as pain, hunger or fear—Sigismund's obsession is of the intellect and, in many ways, he is as near to the "Tyro" species as to the wild bodies. His wish to progress backwards is stronger than most people's to progress forwards, and he becomes an embodiment of his pathological studies. In Sigismund's case, and in the Lewisian taxonomy of obsessions generally, the psychological assumptions are closer to those of the seventeenth and eighteenth century than those of early twentieth-century "alienists." Lewis pursues the Bergsonian "thingness" behind the human façade, and his creatures are reduced to their most dominant character-istics. These caricatures of humanity—as in Ben Jonson's comedy of humours or Pope's presentation of "Ruling Passions"—are personifications. There are many similarities between Lewis's reifications and such simplistic moral psychologies, but his "primitive creatures" and "sun-drunk insects" do not function within a morality framework. Representing nothing beyond themselves, they exist to encourage that human bark called laughter which, wrote Lewis, "is *per se* a healthy clatter" ("Studies in the Art of Laughter," 515).

Lewis wrote several stories with World War I as either setting or backcloth, and in these he looks at social phenomena more sophisticated than the primitive group psychology of the wild bodies. In "The French Poodle" (*The Egoist*, March, 1916), war is presented as one of the "tragic handicaps" of existence which has been exalted into a way of life in modern society. The ever-present threat of death and the first-hand experience of slaughter create "trench scars" in the mind of Rob Cairn. Suffering from shellshock, Cairn is both physically and emotionally scarred. What man has done to man utterly disgusts him; in place of this inhumanity Cairn postulates "the sanity of direct animal processes." But he has been conditioned to brutality; he kills and is killed; there is no escape from the man-made environment of violence.

In *The Wild Body*, Lewis had focused upon primitive—if complex—individuals in primitive environments; in the war stories he looks at the effects of complex—if, ultimately, uncivilized—environments upon the individual. "The King of the Trenches" is the only story of Lewis's to deal directly with life at the Front. It appeared in the second edition of *Blasting and Bombardiering* (1967) and draws on the same experience as is brilliantly recorded in that autobiography. Captain Burney Polderdick is a much-decorated officer in command of a battery of trench mortars, and his exploits are described by Lieutenant Donald Menzies, the Lewis-man of the story. From the outset it is obvious that Polderdick is quite mad—his "eccentricity" having that compulsive power which pushes it beyond acceptable limits. His actions are not always under the control of the rational mind and, in a stressful situation, he becomes a *mélange* of tin-hat and flying limbs. Unlike Cairn, Burney is not viewed as a tragic figure caught in a web of war. He represents, rather, the wild body at war:

> When Polderdick arrived the Line was quiet. A few days afterwards the Trench was constantly shelled. Polderdick was there. They began shelling with shrapnel. At the first patter of the shrapnel Polderdick dived headlong into a dug-out, but his tin-hat

crashed with great force against the tin-hat of an infantry captain who was darting out at the moment. They both disappeared, Polderdick's buttocks revolving as he fell inside. (173)

Polderdick's deranged "Ha! *Ha!*" is yet another category in Lewis's anatomy of laughter: it is the explosion of a mind signalling its unwillingness to adhere to that consensus of opinion called reality. Polderdick's insanity consists of an idiosyncratic restructuring of experience and the creation of a new reality in which he becomes "King of a terrible narrow kingdom."

"I am the King of the Trenches!" he shouted. "Didn't you know who I was? Yes! I am Burney Polderdick, the king of the Trenches! —Ha! *Ha!*" He flourished his stick, twirled it lightly, lunged forward, and dug the Colonel in the middle of the stomach. (182)

There is a sympathetic attractiveness about Menzies's account of Polderdick, as if he senses that this wild body madness is no more insane, and certainly less dangerous, than the madness of war. Polderdick, however, is transferred to a Training Depot in England, and his demented reign ends in exile.

As *Blasting and Bombardiering* illustrates only too well, war can have the effect of dehumanizing men until they become mere cogs in the great impersonal war-machine. Yet, in the Bergsonian sense of people behaving like things, this dehumanizing can still be seen as comic. Lewis's description of the West Indian sergeant (in *Blasting and Bombardiering*) presents him as a lithe man-machine who returns to his post as automatically and exactly as shells find the breech:

At our Nieuport position one dark night the negroes were rolling shells up to the guns—very large ones, since the guns were outsize. This operation had to be effected without so much as a match struck, lest the German air patrols should spot us. A negro sergeant I noticed was not only stationary, and peculiarly idle, but actually obstructing the work of the dusky rollers. I spoke to him. He neither looked at me nor answered. I could scarcely see him—it was very dark, and he was dark. I ordered him to do a little rolling. This was a *word of command*. It elicited no response from the dark shape. Whereupon I gave him a violent push. This propelled him through space for a short distance, but he immediately returned to where he had stood before. I gave him a second push. As if made of india-rubber, he once more reintegrated the spot he had just left. After this I accepted him as part of the landscape, and the shells had to be rolled round him, since they could not be rolled *through* him. (152–153)

Soldiers as part of the landscape, the gigantic guns and shells as alive as they—or the soldiers as thing-like as their guns—are features of many of Lewis's war paintings. Caught in mid-action, the soldiers in the background of "A Battery Shelled" (1919) are transfixed in static geometrical positions reminiscent of the figures of Lewis's Vorticist period. These puny metallic shapes, labouring to the massive totemic guns which block out the sky, are sometimes indistinguishable from the ammunition stock-piled beside them. Like the palm of a gigantic hand, the earth is ploughed and furrowed, far more vital than the transmogrified humanity it grasps. The three figures loitering in the foreground of the painting are more realistically portrayed and have an air of authority. Apparently disengaged from the hellish activity continuously grinding on below them, they are more in control, more withdrawn, not so involved in the destructive machine and hence better able to observe its functions. This "outsider" position is everywhere stressed by Lewis, and through his Cantleman *persona* in *Blasting and Bombardiering* he sums it up thus:

> In the first days (after the declaration of war) he experienced nothing but a penetrating interest in all that was taking place. His detachment was complete and his attention was directed everywhere. (77)

In the original Cantleman story, "Cantleman's Spring-Mate" which first appeared in *The Little Review* (October 1917), the war is in the background, but casts its shadow over all "ordinary" life. Cantleman is an infantry officer who is on leave, but, about to depart to the Front for the first time, "his thoughts and sensations all had, as a philosophic background, the prospect of death." Played out against this threat of cataclysmic violence, every action has about it a tenseness and a sense of urgency. Like the eponymous hero of *Tarr*, Cantleman is a Kerr-Orr figure who, while all too aware of the limitations of his fellow men, aspires to *übermensch* status—and fails. Perceiving that violence is inherent in all life, that both Nature *and* humanity are red in

61

tooth and claw, Cantleman attempts to defeat life at its own game.

His body feels itself at one with wild Nature and is beguiled by the sensuality of spring; his mind is appalled at the body's grossness and its desire to be part of "the madness of natural things." Cantleman is Cartesian man *par excellence*: combining the traits of both wild body and laughing observer, he observes his own desires in action. "Dissecting his laugh," he compares it to the pig's grunt; without the intellect the wild body would be free to rut with the abandon of pigs, but man is *animal capax rationis* and hence aware of his own absurdity. It is upon Stella, his spring mate and Nature's agent, that Cantleman wreaks his revenge. By humiliating her, he believes, he will be undermining a natural and universal order that is both grotesque and brutal. Stella is a young country girl, quite unaware of the complex reactions she has loosed in her lover. She awakes in him "all the sensations he had been divining in the creatures around him, the horse, the bird and the pig." His relationship with her satisfies both the "gnawing yearning in his blood" and, paradoxically, his wish for revenge upon a Nature which makes him feel such desires. Acting towards Stella "with as much falsity as he could master," his calculated seduction of Nature's "agent" is an attempt to outwit her "hostile power." Remaining "deliberate and aloof," through the medium of Stella, Cantleman feels he is raping Nature:

> On the warm earth consent flowed up into her body from all the veins of the landscape. That night he spat out, in gushes of thick delicious rage, all the lust that had gathered in his body. The nightingale sang ceaselessly in the small wood at the top of the field where they lay. He grinned up towards it, and once more turned to the devouring of his mate. He bore down on her as though he wished to mix her body into the soil, and pour his seed into a more methodless matter, the brown phalanges of floury land. As their two bodies shook and melted together, he felt that he was raiding the bowels of Nature. (Reprinted in Calder and Boyars' *Blasting and Bombardiering*, 310)

The complexity of Cantleman's desire for Stella, his hatred for his own weakness, and the ambiguous attractiveness of his revenge, are all allusively conveyed in the violent imagery of intercourse.

In his mood of "impartial malignity," Cantleman feels that he has won the laurels in his vendetta with Nature, but the whole tenor of the writing denies this. Far from disrupting the pattern of Nature, he plays an integral part in every stage of the natural progression of copulation, birth and—when beating out a German's brains—death. Cantleman's callous and vicious treatment of Stella is an attempt to defeat Nature on her own amoral terms and thus, by remaining above the processes, avoid the "souillure." But the story reveals the insufficiency of the Nietzschean concept of "Will" in this struggle: it is impossible to remain "indifferent to Nature's threat," even when the essence of this threat is intellectually recognized. To be in life is to be tainted by life; this is the lesson learned by so many of Lewis's Supermen *manqués*, and only Pierpoint in *The Apes of God*, by eremetically withdrawing from life, manages to function successfully as disembodied mind.

Where the early *Wild Body* stories presented idiosyncratic characters and conflicts illustrative of human psychology, "Cantleman's Spring-Mate" presents conflicts which embody ideas. Published the year after "Cantleman," "The War Baby" (*Art and Letters*, Winter 1918), pursues similar concepts against a similar wartime background; but Richard Beresin, the soldier-protagonist, is much more of a buffoon than Cantleman. Beresin's ideals are not the product of strenuous philosophy, but were bred from the "tenacious middle class snobberies" of public school, nurtured by Paris, Huysmans and Nietzsche, and now—tended by a "soldier-servant"—are in full flower. A puppet driven by subjective dreams, Beresin inhabits an idealistic realm cut off from the real world by snobbish illusions. His grandiose vision invades—indeed submerges—reality with the Nietzschean equivalent of Romanticism. Charlie Peace, The Brides in the Bath, Oscar Wilde, Huysmans, together with Nietzsche, all romp promiscuously in Beresin's idiot pantheon, and are responsible for his delusions of grandeur. In the Prologue to the first edition of *Tarr* (1918), Lewis diagnoses the Nietzschean cult which has produced "the ungainliest and strangest aristocratic caste any world could hope to see":

In Europe Nietzsche's gospel of desperation, the beyond-the-law-man etc., has deeply influenced the Paris apache, the Italian

Futuriste *litterateur*, the Russian revolutionary. Nietzsche's books are full of seductions and sugar-plums. They have made aristocrats of people who would otherwise have been only mild snobs or meddlesome prigs . . . they have made an Over-man of every vulgarly energetic grocer in Europe. (x)

Like Cantleman, Beresin represents a critique of his philosophy. In different ways, both are attempting to live out their ideologies and impose their own patterns upon existence; but once translated into action, ideas lose their purity and become tainted by the imperfections of humanity. In a similar manner, John Porter Kemp, the central character of Lewis's dialectical drama *The Ideal Giant* (1917), propounds a philosophy of extreme action which, however coherently expressed, is shown to be, in practice, totally ludicrous. Kemp's conversations represent his groping towards a satisfactory personal philosophy, and he concludes that conventional behaviour, because mechanical, should be shunned. However, what is intellectually valid and clear-cut can, in action, become chaotic and vague. Philosophy has no law beyond itself, whereas life is hedged in with a multitude of contingencies which blur the edges of ideal forms. When Kemp's "philosophy of action" is put into practice the result is a bizarre emblematic comment upon his original ethic.

Kemp tells Rose that "honesty is a rhythm; it must be broken up," and the important thing is to act positively (instead of merely "playing"):

> "My point is plain. It is entirely a question of whole hogging, and escaping from the dreariness and self-contempt of *play*. We *play* at everything here—at love, art, winning and losing—don't we? . . . Yet *action*, if you could find the right action, is the 'sovereign cure for our ills'. . . . Any wildly subversive action should be welcomed. *We must escape from the machine in ourselves! Smash it up: renew ourselves.*"

The insistence upon a cataclysmic personal violence beyond the bounds of good and evil is distinctly Nietzschean. Kemp is disgusted with his own puny attempts to break the conventional rhythm of honesty and confound a mundane reality with lies. Similarly, believing that Rose has stolen some spoons as a symbolic act, Kemp tells her that such gesturing is merely playing at desperation:

"I feel that my lies and your spoons were about as playful as some of the absurdities with which we reproach our art friends. Compared to death on a barricade, or the robber Garnier's Swedish exercises while he was in hiding in the suburbs of Paris, they are slight exploits. The blood that spurts from a tapped proboscis is not enough. A spoon will not thrust you into jail for so long that you forget what the Earth looks like. For the hair to turn white, the heart to turn grey, in an hour, you require the real thing, ma mie."

But, unknown to Kemp, Rose *has* committed herself in the manner set forth by him: she has killed her father. Touched with blood-stained hands, philosophy has become sullied. As a policeman attempts to apprehend Rose, the play ends with a ludicrous scramble of bodies on the floor of the cafe.

In *The Ideal Giant* Lewis treats important themes through a veil of heavy irony. It is as if he finds, like Kerr-Orr who is "*never* serious about anything," that even momentous issues are Janus-faced and are forever pushing forward their absurd aspect. Kemp's philosophizing is, on one level, an attempt to hammer out what Lewis in *The Art of Being Ruled* calls a "working system of thought." Lewis manages to catch that nice balance between recognizing the importance of Kemp's attempt, while, at the same time, satirizing it most savagely. With Rose's arrest Kemp achieves his mock *anagnorosis*; the folly of his *übermensch* idealism is revealed. It is doubly ironical that Kemp should have learned, not through the folly of his own Dostoevskyan extravagance, but through the actions of a female *doppelgänger*. Throughout the play Kemp believes that he is playing Raskolnikov to Rose's Sonia, but finally he discerns that, in fact, the roles have been reversed.

Cantleman, Beresin, Kemp—all are defeated by life. They do assert positives, but the fiction is an embodiment of their inadequacy rather than their validity. Almost as an answer to the *mauvaise foi* of these characters, the fictional Benjamin Richard Wing lays down his premises for the good life in "The Code of a Herdsman" (*The Little Review*, July 1917). Just as the first versions of the *Wild Body* stories showed Lewis exalting argument above design, so "The Code" represents a fictional presentation of ideas without plot or character. In the form of a letter, this epistolary dramatic monologue is a short but comprehensive set of rules for the avoidance of "the obscenities of existence" and the type of social contacts which dogged the other failed "Natures." Wing is quite dogmatic in his assertions: Mankind and the Exceptional Man cannot coexist and so the only answer is a rigidly divisive Olympian life-style for the "Herdsmen" or "Mountain people." The deliberately extravagant irony of the piece does not mask the seriousness of intent: "The Code" contains the seeds of the Manichean vision of *The Art of Being Ruled*, Pierpoint's Encyclicals in *The Apes of God*, and Lewis's own "Enemy" *persona*. The *sine qua non* of Wing's argument rests upon the assumption that humanity can be divided, on the one hand, into "Herd" and, on the other, into "Mountain people" or "Herdsmen." It is also understood that any trafficking with the "Yahooesque and rotten herd" must be distasteful in the extreme:

> Spend some of your spare time every day in hunting your weaknesses, caught from commerce with the herd, as methodically, solemnly and vindictively as a monkey uses with his fleas. You will find yourself swarming with them while you are surrounded by humanity. But you must not bring them up onto the mountain. . . . Do not play with political notions, aristocratisms or the reverse, for that is a compromise with the herd. Do not allow yourself to imagine "a fine herd, though still a herd." There is no *fine herd*. The cattle that call themselves "gentlemen" you will observe to be a little cleaner. It is merely cunning and produced with a product of combined soda and fats. But you will find no serious difference between them and those vast dismal herds they avoid.

The basis of this elitism is ontological not social and, like Plato's exaltation of the Philosopher-King, proceeds from an unquestioned acceptance of the primacy of the intellect. The arrogant Mosaic tone of the piece is brilliantly sustained throughout, and much of the sardonic humour derives from the straight-faced precision with which the allegory is pursued:

> *There are very stringent regulations* about the herd keeping off the sides of the mountain. In fact your chief function is to prevent this happening. Some in moments of boredom, or vindictiveness,

66

are apt to make rushes for the higher regions. Their instinct always fortunately keeps them in crowds or bands, and their trespassing is soon noticed.

The inhumanity of the attitude lies in the deliberate confusion of image and reality: "herd" gradually loses its metaphorical sense and the "Yahoos of the plain" are spoken of, quite literally, as animals. "The terrible processions beneath," writes Wing from the heights, "are not of our making, and are without our pity." This superb egotism reduces others to mere functions of the self, and one is reminded of Kerr-Orr's confession in *The Wild Body*:

> I admit that I am disposed to forget that people are real—that they are, that is, not subjective patterns belonging specifically to me, in the course of this joke-life, which indeed has for its very principle a denial of the accepted actual. (4)

Wing looks upon humanity with all the indifference that Joyce characterized as central to the aesthetic attitude. Paring his fingernails, Wing does not "forget" the reality of others—he *denies* it. Yet, apart from Pierpoint, Lewis's characters never long endure the rarified air of the Mountain (even Wing has "a pipe below sometimes"), and a recurrent theme throughout the fiction is just this conflict between the concepts of the Mountain and the exigencies of the Plain.

3

The Famous Feeling of Indifference

According to Lewis's preface to the 1918 edition of *Tarr*, his first novel was begun in 1907 when he was living and working mainly on the Continent. The material was reworked several times before January 1916 when he wrote to his friend, Captain Guy Baker:

> I have written an extremely good book, a novel called *Tarr*. I spent £15 on the typing and retyping of it. The idiot Lane (who published *Blast*) says it is "too strong a book" for the present time. To my amazement I find it is difficult to place it. Disarray to all my calculations!—Now. I *must* get it out by hook or by crook. I will vouch that there is nothing in it that the Police could get a prosecution on. I vouch also that a thousand people in London would read it, eventually many more. I know it is a sound book. . . . I am on the threshold of my military career, and have to settle this business for money reasons, before I can enlist. (*Letters*,74–75)

Lane's fears of prosecution could well have been due to the successful action against *The Rainbow* the previous December, but Lewis's difficulties ended later that month when Harriet Shaw Weaver, at Ezra Pound's intercession, accepted *Tarr* for serial publication in *The Egoist*. The Pound-Weaver combination had also been responsible for the serialization of Joyce's *A Portrait of the Artist as a Young Man* just prior to *Tarr*, and in 1919 they were also to publish sections from Joyce's *Ulysses*. With the £50 Lewis received for serial rights he eventually settled his affairs, put his belongings in store, and enlisted in the British Army as "71050 Gunner W. Lewis."

The serial began in April 1916—a month after Lewis joined up —and ran until November 1917, Lewis receiving his copies in the trenches. The novel, with few minor revisions, was finally published in book-form in July 1918 by *The Egoist*. Those chapters omitted from the serial for lack of space were replaced, the syntax of some foreign phrases was corrected, and some proper names were changed. More important, the prologue was considerably expanded, drawing attention to Tarr's "philosophy." It was this over-insistence upon the thesis (in what was so obviously a *roman à thèse*) that T. Sturge-Moore, one of Lewis's earliest mentors and admirers, saw as quite needless:

> "I never see Tarr as I do the German and I find a difficulty in swallowing some of your artificially prepared talk about him," wrote Sturge-Moore to Lewis in September 1918. "I wish he had either been more frankly you or more wholly distinct from his creator. . . . I rather regret the preface and epilogue; they will distract reflection from the book itself to the doctrine it will be supposed to illustrate, which is far from being so sound or certain a thing. They are like a rope anchoring it to Pound's Little World, whereas it might sail the blue quite unattached with advantage." (*Letters*, 99)

The gist of these criticisms—that Tarr's mask too often slips and reveals his creator—was felt by Lewis himself. He saw Tarr as "too much of (his) mouthpiece," and the prolegomenous sections do deliberately draw attention to the fact that many of Tarr's ideas are also those of Lewis. In the serialized "Epilogue," Lewis states explicitly:

> I associate myself with all (Tarr) says on the subject of humour. In fact I put him up to it. He is one of my showmen. (*The Egoist*, November 1917, 153)

Despite an awareness that Tarr is "a caricatural self-portrait of sorts" (*Rude Assignment*, 151), a cathartic writing-out of early experiences, and that the ideas of Tarr and Lewis are often identical, the novel still has aesthetic coherence *qua* novel. As an exemplary figure, Tarr embodies many of the positives of his creator and "is intended to bring some comfort of analysis among less sifted and more ominous perplexities of our time. His message as he discourses, laughs, picks his way through the heavily obstructed land of this story, is the message of a figure of health" (1918, xi). Yet these ideas and attitudes are assimilated into the fictional world of the novel, they function within it without

69

reference to Lewis, and it is not the case—as Sturge-Moore and later critics have suggested—that to reject the ideas of Tarr/Lewis is to reject the novel.

Tarr poses and tentatively answers questions about the type of sexual relationships suitable for the artist. Tarr vacillates between the "lumpen sex" of Bertha and the aesthetically pleasing "swagger sex" of Anastasya. The question is viewed from all sides; Tarr is even provided with an *alter ego* (in Kreisler) so that the converse of the proposition can be explored. Tarr, an English painter living in Paris, decides—after rationally surveying his sexual finances— to leave his German mistress Bertha Lunken because he is "humanizing sex too much." Yet, feeling that a clean break would be very difficult for him, he plans a self-imposed aversion therapy; he "doses" himself liberally and carefully tends his *ennui*. Tarr is greatly attracted to Anastasya Vasek, a totally different type to Bertha: she is intelligent where Bertha is slow witted; classically beautiful rather than vulgarly sensuous; and an individual where Bertha is a born slave. Otto Kreisler, a penniless German artist, complicates the clear-cut dealings between Tarr and his women. Kreisler is infatuated with Anastasya and when baulked both in love and finance, he fights a ridiculous duel, kills his opponent by mistake and later commits suicide, leaving Bertha expecting his child. Though Tarr now lives with Anastasya, he marries Bertha to save her honour. Without fail, he sees Bertha from 4 p.m. until seven, and Anastasya for the remainder of the day. However, when Tarr grows tired of the latter's beautiful perfection, he takes another Bertha-type. When he tires of *her* there is another like Anastasya and, it seems, so on.

Tarr stands as a touchstone against whom all the other characters and their ideas are weighed. Central to his own philosophy is the notion that "Humour," the great vice of the English, is both phoney and harmful, and should be eschewed. Like the *übermensch* dreams of Beresin, the aristocratic obsessions of Sigismund and the romantic illusions of Margot (in *The Revenge for Love*), "Humour" is a lens which distorts reality:

> "The University of Humour—that is what it is—that prevails everywhere in England for the formation of youth, provides you with nothing but a first-rate means of evading reality. All english training is a system of *deadening feeling*, a stoic prescription—a

humorous stoicism is the anglo-saxon philosophy. Many of the results are excellent: it saves from gush in many cases; in times of crisis or misfortune it is an excellent armour. The english soldier gets his special cachet from that. But for the sake of this wonderful panacea—english humour—the English sacrifice so much. It is the price of empire, if you like. It would be better *to face* our imagination and nerves without this drug. . . . Anyhow, the time seems to have arrived in my life, as I consider it has arrived in the life of the nation, to discard this husk. I'm all for throwing off humour: life must be met on other terms than those of fun and sport now. The time has come. Otherwise—disaster!

". . . I'm going to swear off Humour for a year to set all Englishmen an example. Even upon you, Guy, I shall gaze inhumanly. All these mock matrimonial difficulties of mine come from humour. I'm going to gaze on Bertha inhumanly, and not humorously any longer, that's flat." (*Tarr*, 1928 Version, reprinted by Calder and Boyars, 1968, 32–34)

This concept of humour is far removed from the mind-sneezing "bark of delight" with which Kerr-Orr greeted absurdity. His philosophy of laughter was not an evasion, but rather a recognition of a more profound reality: he glimpsed the depths of the abyss and saw "the grin upon the Deathshead," to which the natural reaction is a convulsive spasm of the intellect. This is the "risus purus" defined by Samuel Beckett as "the laugh of laughs" which salutes the highest joke by laughing at that which is unhappy. At this level, "laughter" is the most fundamental of all philosophical statements and totally removed from the peculiarly English stiff-upper-lip, grin-and-bear-it attitude, which Tarr terms "humour."

Once Tarr decides to replace humour with "indifference," his affairs with Bertha take on the simple inevitability of a syllogism. The insidious "lymphatic" attraction that Bertha had for him—suggesting a physically strangling biological grasp—is rationalized out of existence. In the light of reason all Tarr's difficulties vanish; the clear lines of logical propositions with their neat Q.E.D.s cut through the slop and romance of his relationship. Acting as a foil to Tarr, Kreisler is an extrapolation of his former attitude: as Tarr withdraws from the welter of sensuality, the German, as if a mirror image, becomes more deeply immersed in the mire of his own and others' emotions. Tarr's every action is filtered through the self-conscious intellect: Kreisler personifies

71

impulsive action. They are the two limbs of the novel's dialectic and its structure reinforces this opposition. The novel opens with Tarr meeting Hobson and talking; meeting Butcher and talking; seeking out Lowndes and talking. Gradually formulating his decision to leave, he finally delivers his ultimatum to Bertha. The whole process is diagrammatically structured in clear, hard-edged lines. Those events involving Kreisler, on the other hand, are characterized by their untidy sprawl. Acting independently of his reason, Kreisler's emotional life, like a runaway automaton, takes over. The visit to the Bonnington Club, the rape, the bloody fiasco of the duel—all result from Kreisler's inability to deal with reality. He feels antagonized by the circumambient flux and his spontaneous reaction is to thrash out in all directions as, in a welter of violent action, he attempts to revenge himself upon existence.

Just as Tarr withdraws from those attitudes represented by Kreisler and the English vice of "humour," so too does he reject the sophisticated herd-mindedness of Alan Hobson. This complex of group ideas—"the lees of liberalism, the poor froth blown off the decadent nineties, and the wardrobe leavings of a vulgar bohemianism"—has an off-the-peg set of value-judgments, a "mental outfit" to fit any occasion. Tarr flees such collective security and, stepping beyond the bounds of conventional behaviour, becomes an outsider beholden to none and responsible only to himself.

Although Tarr tells Anastasya that he is " 'the new animal . . . the thing that will succeed the superman,' " there are certain Nietzschean traits in his arrogance. Yet the premises underlying this philosophy proceed from his aesthetic ideals rather than from anything resembling a "will to power." The artist, Tarr postulates, as creative being, has a unique relationship with reality, and it is this—uncluttered by extraneous considerations or the contingent chaos of life—that Tarr seeks to approximate in his everyday relationships. It is implicit in the novel that, being an artist, Tarr is different from the rest of humanity: normal standards and morës do not apply; his art alone is of supreme importance; all else peripheral. With the artist the normal drives—the Freudian "libido"—before finding satisfaction in sexual activity, are channelled first into the aesthetically perfect realm of art. Thus, in terms of this psychology of creativity, all Tarr needs from Bertha is physical satisfaction—a form of sexual hygiene. " 'A lonely phallus,' " Tarr tells Hobson, is the " 'one solitary thing left facing any woman with whom (the artist) has commerce' " (18). When he feels that sexuality is becoming tainted by a vulgar romanticism, this is the point at which to sharpen up his indifference.

Feeling himself caught in Bertha's cloying web of sentimental sensuality, Tarr hoists the *"famous feeling of indifference"* as consciously as he would a *papier mâché* mask. As he approaches Bertha's salon it is obvious that he is in alien territory; her taste is typically "bourgeois-bohemian":

> Green silk cloth and cushions of various vegetable and mineral shades covered everything, in mildewy blight. The cold repulsive shades of Islands of the Dead, gigantic cypresses, grottoes of teutonic nymphs, had installed themselves massively in this french flat. Purple metal and leather steadily dispensed with expensive objects. There was a plaster-cast of Beethoven (some people who have frequented artistic circles get to dislike this face extremely), brass jars from Normandy, a photograph of Mona Lisa (Tarr could not look upon the Mona Lisa without a sinking feeling). (44)

Bertha's physical environment—like a turgid still-life—defines her character. Like Kreisler, "her emotions are too much part of her intelligence," and Tarr is sickened by her frequent and impassioned "psychic discharges." His indifference relegates (or exalts) all experience to an aesthetic plane, and it is solely upon such amoral grounds that actions are evaluated. When Bertha breaks into tears, Tarr is only interested in the observable phenomena and their aesthetic value. That Bertha is upset is quite irrelevant:

> Women's psychic discharges affected him invariably like the sight of a person being sea-sick. It was the result of a weak spirit, as the other was the result of a weak stomach, they could only live on the retching seas of their troubles on the condition of being quite empty. (53)

As Tarr later explains in his diatribe on aesthetics: " 'The eye alone sees nothing at all but conventional phantoms,' " and the intellect interprets sense-data according to socially inculcated

73

models. At a stroke, Tarr throws off all set responses, all comforting illusions and—as if experiencing everything for the first time—his intellect faces reality without the *mauvaise foi* of conventional patterns of thought or behaviour. Bertha's sobbing evokes no emotive connotations or responses, but strikes Tarr as being "like the buzzing on a comb covered with paper." Similarly, "with the attentiveness that a man bestows to his chin after a shave, in little, brusque, hard strokes," Bertha dries her eyes. This is observation unhampered by that lens which arranges "reality" into socially acceptable *gestalts*, and, as such, it is closer to a camera eye than a human one. Tarr, without the distorting lens of "humour," sees Bertha as a "high grade Aryan bitch" and this new attitude gives his intellect *carte blanche* to solve his problems according to its own dictates.

This inhuman, non-personal vision resulting from Tarr's "indifference" is, in many ways, similar to Lewis's own descriptive technique in his fiction. After the duel, for instance, the flight of Bitzenko and Kreisler from the scene of the killing is related as if human locomotion were being observed for the first time:

> Calling "run!" to Kreisler, (Bitzenko) took to his heels, followed by his compatriot—whose neck shot in and out and whose great bow legs could almost be heard twanging as he ran. They reached another hedge, ran along the farther side of it, Bitzenko bent double as though to escape a rain of bullets. (257)

Many of the startlingly original images of emotional states derive from Lewis's trick of presenting shades of feeling by concrete analogies. Tarr's sense of being trapped by Bertha's ultrasensitivity is brilliantly realized in a grotesquely tactile coleopterous image:

> An intense atmosphere of teutonic suicide permeated everything: he could not move an eyelid or a muscle without wounding or slighting something: it was like being in a dark kitchen at night, where you know at every step you will put your foot upon a beetle—there was indeed a still closer analogy to this in the disgust he felt for these too naked and familiar things upon which he was treading. (289)

Such imagery, by means of semantic gravitation, demotes the life of the emotions to a ridiculous sub-world in which the artist becomes involved at his peril. In *Men Without Art* (1934), Lewis states this view without the comic overtones; it is a hard, ascetic philosophy:

> The sentient world is dross. It is ugly dross, as well, contorted throughout its length and breadth by the foolish grimaces into which the vulgar soul within the flesh churns it up, in yahoo laughter, or creases it, with a sly grin or simper. (228)

In *Tarr*, this same "Classical" asperity underlies the bizarre comedy of sexual relationships, and the extravagant objective correlatives for inner states are a *reductio ad absurdum* of the sentient world:

> Soltyk's death dismayed (Kreisler) deeply: if you will think of a demented person who has become possessed of the belief that it is essential for the welfare of the world that he should excuperate into a bird's nest while standing upon one leg on the back of a garden seat, but who is baulked, first of all by the seat giving way, and secondly by the bird's nest catching fire and vanishing because of the use by the bird of certain chemical substances in its construction, combined with the heat of the sun, you will have a parallel for Kreisler's superstitious disappointment. (259)

Lewis's method of presenting cerebral and emotional *modus operandi* is antithetical to the "stream of consciousness" technique. He does not attempt to convey the processes of the thinking mind, but rather solidifies and externalizes the mental flux into a clearly defined progression of *tableaux vivants*. The difference between Tarr and Kreisler is that the former's reason controls the card-index system of stimulus-response, while, like a randomly programmed computer, the latter is at its mercy. Tarr is one of the most self-aware characters in literature and his attempt to replace *id* by *ego* is, in his terms, a success. His "indifference" does not spring from a situation—as emotions are wont to do—but is brought to the situation. Before meeting Bertha, he gave "a hasty glance at his 'indifference' to see whether it were O.K.," and the "thinking part" of his mind is constantly observing and arranging the "feeling part." As if magnified and projected by a magic-lantern, psychic processes are transformed into visual images and coolly observed by Tarr. When he offers to marry Bertha because she is expecting Kreisler's child, his schizoid mind reacts in two ways: "the indignant plebs" of the emotions are aghast, but the intellect, seeing the joke, defends its decision. The result of the conflict, as palpable as an animated battle between red and white corpuscles, is never in doubt:

> The indignant plebs of his glorious organism rioted around his mind.
>
> "Ah-ha! Ah-ha! dirty practical joker, dirty intellect, where are you leading us now?" They were vociferous. "You have kept us fooling in this neighbourhood so long and now you are pledging us to your fancy fool forever. Ah-ha! Ah-ha!"
>
> A faction clamoured "Anastasya!" Certain sense-sections attacked him in vulnerable spots with Anastasya's voluptuous banner unfurled and fragrant. He buffeted his way along, as though spray were dashing in his face, watchful behind his glasses. He met his thoughts with a contemptuous stiff veteran smile: this capricious and dangerous master had an offensive stylistic coolness, similar to Wellington breakfasting at Salamanca while Marmont hurried exultingly into traps: they were of the same metal, enemies and demagogues and haters of the mob. (292)

A technique related to Lewis's presentation of the human in terms of inanimate matter, is his Dickensian practice of investing lifeless objects with a wild vitality. The Restaurant Vallet, for instance, like a monstrous termite, works its way into surrounding rooms with a strange, threatening vigour:

> As trade grew the small business had burrowed backwards into the ramshackle house: bursting through walls and partitions, flinging down doors, it discovered many dingy rooms in the interior that it hurriedly packed with serried cohorts of eaters. It had driven out terrified families, had hemmed the apoplectic concierge in her "loge," it had broken out on to the court at the back in shed-like structures: and in the musty bowels of the house it had established a broiling luridly lighted roaring den, inhabited by a fierce band of slatternly savages. (88)

In "Unlucky for Pringle" the same sort of non-human energy is evinced when the contents of Pringle's portmanteau scatter themselves about his room "like a flock of birds and pack of dogs, the brushes dashing to the dressing-table, the photographs crowding to the chimneypiece, the portmanteaus, boxes, and parcels creeping under the bed and into corners." Fitting into this pattern of cosmic dynamism, Chalaran in "Pringle" and Kreisler, "the nursery locomotive," both partake of the same thing-like energy. Like the startling *imagiste* metaphors in "The Enemy of the Stars," Lewis yokes together dissimilars in characteristic manner. Bertha's complex emotions on seeing Kreisler, for instance, are allusively expressed with the compression of a *haiku* and with suggestions of things-as-persons and persons-as-things:

> (Kreisler) stared up at the house with eager speculation: he examined the house and studio opposite. Behind the curtains Bertha stood with the emotions of an ambushed sharp-shooter; she felt on her face the blankness of the house wall, all her body was as unresponsive as the brick: the visitor beneath appeared almost to be looking at her face, magnified and exposed, instead of at the walls of the house and its windows. (169)

In *Rude Assignment* Lewis looks back to the first edition of *Tarr*: "It was," he admits, "a very carelessly written book indeed. That criticism does not apply to the revised version (1928)." Expanding, omitting or rewriting whole sections to clarify motivation or shift emphasis, Lewis eliminated all signs of hasty composition. No page is without a dozen syntactical alterations. Hugh Kenner feels that the later version loses some of its "sensuous primitive energy" and that the revised locutions "signify less when brushed off for the market than when streaked with the loam of the unconscious from which they were so hastily gathered" (37). But in teasing out the implications of his images, a much more solid, visual world emerges. Plain statements of fact are filled out, usually with an eye for those details which add an ironic edge to the facts:

> A man she knew, now in the Midi, sent her now and then a few francs. (1918, 102)

In revision this becomes:

> In the Midi at present, a substantial traveller in pharmaceutical goods, who had enjoyed her earliest transports in the days when she worked at Arras, sent her a few francs at irregular intervals. (101)

Similarly, Bertha the "high class Aryan female" (1918, 23) is even more trenchantly dismissed as "a high-grade aryan bitch" (29). Pursuing the allusions of the imagery, Lewis gives a fillip to the style. Tarr, "feeling like a bad actor" (1918, 208) when faced with Bertha, feels like "an untalented Pro on a provincial first night" (198) in the revised form: the expanded image suggesting even deeper realms of apprehension. All these stylistic revisions show Lewis picking his words—as he suggested in an interview that the writer should—with the same care as "Frederick the Great picked a tall, fine-chested Pomeranean for his Grenadiers."

Just as Kreisler and Tarr are antithetical and complementary figures in the polemical design of the novel, so too are Bertha and Anastasya. Representing the Romantic/Classical distinction, Bertha is a "mess" while Anastasya is "a clean solid object." Tarr considers that a relationship with Anastasya would combine normal sexual mechanics with an added bonus: "you get a respectable human being into the bargain." Anastasya comprehends and shares Tarr's notions of "pure sex" without the Bertha-like sentimental accoutrements. There is no hint of "ugly sentient dross" about Anastasya: she is a magnificent sexual machine which Tarr desires to take to pieces, "bit by bit, and penetrate to its intimacy." Like Tarr, her sensuality is controlled by reason without being diminished. Together they de-romanticize sex, and Anastasya talks of her own physical being in butcher's shop imagery:

> [Anastasya] lifted up her breast a little way in the palm of her proud hand. "What would you do under the circumstances, Tarr— it's a handicap, there's no blinking the fact . . . it's all part of the beastly shop-window—I have to stick frills around them even, just as pork-merchants in their shop-fronts decorate the carcasses of their sucking pigs." (273)

Refusing to observe "a decent emotionality about these coarse mysteries," Tarr and Anastasya confirm their fellow-feeling in this intercourse of intellects. However, this affair proves, ultimately, to be as impossible as that with Bertha: the artist, Tarr asserts, cannot be constricted by long-term relationships and he is doomed to vacillate promiscuously between Berthas and Anastasyas, satisfying his urges (and his ego) according to his needs. Anastasya is altogether too much for Tarr: "he needed an empty vessel to flood with his vitality, and not an equal and foreign vitality to coldly exist side by side with." As a man, Tarr claims for himself special privileges; as an artist, he claims even more. It is quite acceptable for this "new sort of person, the creative man," to sacrifice women on the altar of his art: "God was man: the woman was a lower form of life."

It does not follow, of course, that all men are god-like, and Kreisler is a perfect example of the wild body species. "The book should have been called *Otto Kreisler*," wrote Lewis in *Rude Assignment*, "rather than *Tarr*, who is a secondary figure." In attempting to account for the "superior vitality of the Kreisler sections," Hugh Kenner points to Lewis's interests being "more profoundly, if not more intensely engaged with Kreisler and his fate than with Tarr's ideas" (43). There is, however, a sense in which Kreisler is very much part of these ideas: he is the embodiment of the converse of Tarr's philosophy. Both Tarr and Kreisler are, on one level, ideas in action, and the novel as a whole exemplifies T. E. Hulme's notion that "it is in taking a concrete example of the working out of a principle in action that you can get its best definition" (*Speculations*). Tarr and Kreisler move in opposite directions around Bertha and Anastasya in a complex, formal dance. The two men are "doubles": the one is all that the other is not. When "sex surged up and martyrized Tarr, he held it down . . . to escape these persecutions he worked incessantly" (188). Kreisler, on the other hand, cannot "hold it down," cannot channel the violence of his libidinous energies into art, but thrusts them out into life and onto women—"that vast dumping ground for sorrow and affliction." Tarr comes to a compromise between art and life which satisfies him: Kreisler, however is unable to manage such an adjustment:

> "This is my theory," says Tarr about Kreisler, "I believe that all the fuss he made was an attempt to get out of Art back into Life again. He was like a fish floundering about who had got into the wrong tank. *Back into sex* I think would describe where he wanted to get to: he was doing his best to get back into sex again out of a little puddle of art where he felt he was gradually expiring." (281)

Tarr's ideas elucidate the complex *rationale* behind characters' behaviour and also provide a framework within which they function as "principles in action."

This analysis of the conflict between art and life is crucial in any reading which stresses the polemical design of the novel. " 'Life is art's rival in all particulars. They are *de puntos* for ever and ever,' " Tarr tells Anastasya:

> "Deadness is the first condition of art. The armoured hide of the hippopotamus, the shell of the tortoise, feathers and machinery, you may put in one camp; naked pulsing and moving of the soft inside of life—along with elasticity of movement and consciousness —that goes in the opposite camp. Deadness is the first condition for art: the second is absence of soul, in the human and sentimental sense. With the statue its lines and masses are its soul, no restless inflammable ego is imagined for its interior: it has *no inside*: good art must have no inside : that is capital." (280)

Seeing art as "life with all the humbug of living taken out of it," Tarr attempts to create this same Classical perfection in his own *life*; as he looks "indifferently" upon existence his value-judgments are based on an extrapolation of these aesthetic criteria. Bertha, for instance, is all "inside"; yet Anastasya's statuesque beauty is made up of "lines and masses." Kreisler, who stumbled into painting by chance, mistakes life for art and, with the violence of a *fauve*, he executes his *tachiste* works with reality as his medium:

> Womenkind were Kreisler's Theatre, they were for him art and expression: the tragedies played there purged you periodically of the too violent accumulations of desperate life. . . . When the events of his life became too wieldy or overwhelming, he converted them into love; as he might otherwise have done, had he possessed a specialized talent, into some art or another. He was a sculptor— a german sculptor of a mock-realistic and degenerate school—in the strange sweethearting of the "free-life." (93–94)

The characters of *Tarr*, however, are much more than mouth-pieces or embodiments of various attitudes: Kreisler is perhaps Lewis's greatest creation. Like all the wild bodies, his atavistic responses betray the cave-man beneath the twentieth-century exterior. Often described as a machine, he is as much part of the world of objects as of people: "measured by chairs or doors, he was of immoderate physical humanity." Once wound up, there is no stopping him—like "a machine with the momentum of all this old blood and iron that was Otto Kreisler he must go on"—but he cannot cope with the complexity of a life which "did not each day deposit an untidiness that could be whisked off by a Gillette blade, as nature did its stubble."

Lewis's narrative technique keeps the reader at a distance from the sufferings of the German, and as his actions move from the pathetic to the violently absurd, sympathy turns to laughter. In attempting to defeat reality, Kreisler creates a comic analogue to replace it. His ridiculous antic disposition instigates farce after brutal farce into which others are remorselessly drawn. Yet even behind the slapstick, Chaplinesque low comedy of, say, the duel, there is the wild body desperation of a mind at the end of its tether. To laugh at Kreisler's misfortune it is necessary, as Bergson states in *Le Rire*, that there should be a deadening of sympathy for the sufferer:

> The comic demands something like a momentary anaesthesia of the heart. Its appeal is to the intelligence, pure and simple.

By carefully channelling the reader's response, Lewis creates this "anaesthesia of the heart" for the entire novel; without empathy Kreisler's "tragedy" becomes black comedy.

As provocative as the deliberately extreme iconoclasm of *Blast*, Lewis's first novel is a sardonic, witty, intellectually dazzling *kunstlerroman*. "Any idea," wrote Lewis in *Paleface* (1929), "should be regarded as 'sentimental' that is not taken to its ultimate conclusion." In *Tarr*, Lewis takes his protagonist's ideas to their "ultimate conclusion" and, as such, the whole tone of the novel endorses Tarr's approach. The failure of Tarr, the "Reasonable Man," is not a personal one, but points, finally, to the tragic fact underlying all "working systems of thought"—they must function within an absurd existence. His basic premise—that "surrender to a woman was a sort of suicide for an artist"— leads inevitably and "rightly" to his promiscuous conclusion:

> Bertha's child was born, and it absorbed her energies for upwards of a year. It bore some resemblance to Tarr. Tarr's afternoon visits became less frequent. He lived now publicly with his illicit and more splendid bride.
>
> Two years after the birth of the child, Mrs. Tarr divorced him: she then married an eye-doctor and lived with a brooding severity in his company and that of her only child.
>
> Tarr and Anastasya did not marry. They had no children.

Tarr, however, had three children by a lady of the name of Rose Fawcett, who consoled him for the splendours of his "perfect woman." But yet beyond the dim though solid figure of Rose Fawcett, another rises. This one represents the swing back of the pendulum once more to the swagger side. The cheerless and stodgy absurdity of Rose Fawcett required as compensation the painted, fine and enquiring face of Prism Dirkes. (299)

Like Arghol, Kemp and Cantleman, Tarr attempts to organize his life according to ideas. His logic is faultless; his argument valid; but his actions are absurd. Yet Tarr's future relationships are less a comment upon his reasoning, and more upon the tragic inability to escape from the Kreisler in Everyman. As Lewis puts it in "The Meaning of the Wild Body": "There is nothing that is animal (and we as bodies are animal) that is not absurd" (244). To have Tarr succeed would have been an evasion of this basic Lewisian truth.

4

The Malefic Cabal

In a letter to Lady Ottoline Morrell, Lytton Strachey voices his disapproval of Lewis, both as artist and man, tracing Henry Lamb's "beastly mean notions" to his friendship with Lewis. Strachey refers to an early short story Lewis published in *The English Review*:

> It was cleverly done—I could no more have written it than flown—fiendish observation, and very original ideas. Yet the whole thing was disagreeable; the subtlety was curiously crude, and the tone all through more mesquin than can be described. . . . Ugh! The total effect was affreux. Living in the company of such a person would certainly have a deleterious influence on one's moral being. (Holroyd: *Lytton Strachey*, Vol II, 74)

Strachey's "affreux" typifies Bloomsbury's corporate reaction to Lewis—one of horrified rejection and disparagement—the strength of which is only equalled by Lewis's reciprocal hatred of the "malefic cabal" that he described in *Blasting and Bombardiering* as having had "such a destructive influence upon the intellectual life of England." Because their premises for the good life were so intrinsically antithetical, Lewis and Bloomsbury made natural enemies. Lewis's whole manner clashed strongly with the Bloomsbury style—Ezra Pound described him thus:

> Mr. Lewis is restless, turbulent, intelligent, bound to make himself felt. If he had not been a vorticist painter he would have been a vorticist something else. He is a man of sudden illuminating antipathies. . . . A man with this kind of intelligence is bound always to be crashing and opposing and breaking. You cannot be intelligent in that sort of way without being prey to the furies. (*The Egoist*, August 1914, 307)

Compared to the Bloomsbury brand of iconoclasm—achieved through Stracheyesque ironies and subtle understatement—Lewis's flamboyant polemical displays were altogether too crude. While the "lonely old volcano of the Right" erupted violently and sporadically in the vicinity of Bloomsbury, hurtling scathing insults at the "aesthete-politicians" whose world resembled "the afternoon tea-party of a perverse spinster," Bloomsbury turned her back, drew in her skirts, and maintained a stony and sometimes horrified silence.

In *Beginning Again*, Leonard Woolf dates the genesis of "Old Bloomsbury" between 1911 and 1914; his reasons are not cultural or aesthetic, but geographical. It was during these years that this closely-knit group of friends whose "roots and the roots of (whose) friendship were in the University of Cambridge," gravitated towards that area of central London encircling the British Museum. Frank Swinnerton best describes this feature of the intellectual geography of the times:

> Central London is mapped for some forgotten reason into different quarters. Thus Soho . . . is the home of a part of London's foreign population and is a centre for French and Italian restaurants; Belgravia is the old highly fashionable district west of Green Park, Mayfair the extraordinarily aristocratic section north of Piccadilly and east of Hyde Park, and so on. And Bloomsbury . . . lies to the north of New Oxford Street, between Tottenham Court Road upon the one side and Gray's Inn Road upon the other. It is the great quarter for squares and private hotels, straight plain Georgian houses . . . publishers, and, residentially, a kind of bourgeois or aesthetic-bourgeois selectness . . . during and immediately after the First World War it became the spiritual, sometimes actual, home of exiles from Cambridge University. (*The Georgian Literary Scene*, 265)

Just after the war so many of the group were living in Gordon Square that Lytton Strachey wrote to Virginia Woolf: "Very soon I foresee that the whole of the square will become a sort of college." But Bloomsbury never developed into anything that could be identified as a "movement"; there were certain common attitudes, but no overall system or theory to which they all dogmatically adhered. They were a "group" primarily because their social and educational environment had drawn them together:

> The colour of our minds and thought had been given to us by the climate of Cambridge and Moore's philosophy. . . . But we had no common theory, system, or principles which we wanted to convert the world to; we were not proselytizers, missionaries, crusaders, or even propagandists. (*Beginning Again*, 25)

When viewed sympathetically, Bloomsbury's virtues are shown to have sprung from the trust engendered by totally honest "personal relationships." Leonard Woolf states that many of the group were "permanently inoculated with Moore and Moorism," and suggests that the Cambridge philosopher was responsible for whatever common attitude they held. Moore's most famous work, *Principia Ethica*, postulates "personal relationships" and a sense of beauty as the two supreme goods—this, says Woolf, was "embraced with the violence and the passion of youth." The "Bloomsberries" were well-educated, sophisticated, dedicated to the Arts, and placed great stress upon "states of mind" and the spiritual: what Virginia Woolf called "all those human faculties and activities which are over and above our mere existence as living organisms." To the outsider, however, Bloomsbury often presented quite a different image: a closed-shop of effete dilettantes whose incestuous, self-congratulatory pretentiousness represented nothing more than their aristocratic notions of superiority. As Roy Campbell puts it in his "Home Truths on Bloomsbury":

> Of all the clever people round me here
> I most delight in me—
> Mine is the only voice I hear,
> And mine the only face I see.

Critics of Bloomsbury return again and again to their arrogant exclusiveness, and their imperious assumption that they had a monopoly of civilized values. For many, Bloomsbury was like a snobbish club: clannish and intolerant of non-members. The Bloomsbury manner was almost a parody of itself; friends never smiled when shaking hands, their conversation abounded in esoteric private jokes, and the "Bloomsbury voice," modelled on Strachey's piping falsetto, appeared to be the height of artificiality. Their much-vaunted "free thinking," too, has been seen as a rigid adherence to the aesthetically and politically modish values of their coterie. Stephen Spender in *World Within World* defined their creed: "Not to regard the French impressionist and post-impressionist painters as sacrosanct, not to be an agnostic, and in politics a Liberal with Socialist leanings, was to put onself outside Bloomsbury" (140).

Between 1911 and 1914, when Bloomsbury was forming, Lewis was acquainted with several members of the incipient group. He knew Virginia Woolf and was friendly with her brother, Adrian Stephen, with whom he stayed in France. He exhibited at the Second Post-Impressionist exhibition at the Grafton Galleries in October 1912; the show was organized by Roger Fry, and its secretary was Leonard Woolf. Fry and Lewis together visited Gertrude Stein, and in *The Autobiography of Alice B. Toklas* the latter goes so far as to call Lewis one of Fry's "young disciples":

> Gertrude Stein rather liked him. She particularly liked him one day when he came and told all about his quarrel with Roger Fry. Roger Fry had come not many days before and had already told all about it. They told the same story only it was different, very different.

The quarrel was the notorious Omega affair which marked the beginning of Lewis's life-long feud with Fry and hence, by implication, with the rest of Bloomsbury. The Omega Workshops had been started by Fry in July 1913, in an attempt to translate the principles of Post-Impressionism into the decorative and applied arts. The idea was that artists should work anonymously for a fixed wage, producing and executing designs for various household goods and undertaking commissions for interior decoration. One such commission was for the decoration of the "Post-Impressionist Room" at the Daily Mail's Ideal Home Exhibition, which the Omega carried out in the summer of 1913— Lewis doing a small piece of carving. It was only on his return from a holiday in France that Lewis was told that the commission had been specifically intended for himself and Spencer Gore (an artist not associated with the Omega). Lewis believed, from information received, that Fry had deliberately misled him, and misappropriated the prestigious commission for the Omega.

After more than half a century it is difficult to discern the true facts of the affair, but whatever the rights and wrongs of the imbroglio, the upshot was the "Round Robin," sent to all associated with Omega, in which Lewis, together with three other artists, accused Fry of perpetrating a "shabby trick." The circular attacked Fry's character, his aesthetics, and his management of the Omega:

> This mean and ludicrous policy of restraining artists might, perhaps, be justified if the Direction at all fulfilled its function of impresario, but its own shows are badly organised, unfairly managed, closed to much good work for petty and personal reasons, and flooded with the work of well-intentioned friends of the Direction. . . .
>
> As to its tendencies in Art, they alone would be sufficient to make it very difficult for any vigorous art-instinct to long remain under that roof. The Idol is still Prettiness, with its mid-Victorian languish of the neck, and its skin is "greenery-yallery," despite the Post-What-Not fashionableness of its draperies. This family party of strayed and Dissenting Aesthetes, however, were compelled to call in as much modern talent as they could find, to do the rough and masculine work without which they knew their efforts would not rise above the level of a pleasant tea-party, or command more attention. . . .
>
> This enterprise seemed to promise in the opportunities afforded it by support from the most intellectual quarters, emancipation from the middleman-shark. But a new form of fish in the troubled waters of Art has been revealed in the meantime, the Pecksniff-shark, a timid but voracious journalistic monster, unscrupulous, smooth-tongued and, owing chiefly to its weakness, mischievous. (*Letters*, 49–50)

The round robin was circularized in October 1913, and at this time Fry was in France. The running of the Omega was in the hands of Fry's fellow-director Vanessa Bell; from her letters it is not difficult to perceive the flurry the affair caused. As Clive Bell wrote to Roger Fry: "It seems to me just possible that we have all lost our heads over this area row."

Fry kept a dignified silence throughout, believing that any action on his part "would only advertise the gentlemen, who, he sometimes suspected, rather enjoyed advertisement." By the end of October the affair had blown over, and when Fry returned from France it was decided that no further action should be taken. But this was only the beginning of Lewis's campaign, which ranged from abusive references to Fry in letters (Lewis wrote to Clive Bell that he had no wish "to remain longer in the vicinity of a bad shit"), to sporadic public attacks mounted whenever opportunity arose. In his "Review of Contemporary Art" in the second issue of *Blast*, Lewis hits out at the Omega:

> The most abject, anaemic, and amateurish manifestation of this Matisse "decorativeness," or Picasso deadness and bland arrangement, could no doubt be found (if that were necessary or served any useful purpose) in Mr. Fry's curtain and pin cushion factory in Fitzroy Square. (*Blast* No. 2, 41)

The taunt of dilettantism was central to Lewis's attacks: wealthy and untalented amateurs, he felt, had a stranglehold on the commercial side of the arts, making life intolerable for serious professional artists like himself.

Two of the most sustained attacks the Vorticists made upon contemporary culture were on the vogue of Futurism, personified by the larger-than-life figure of Marinetti, and upon the precious dilettantism of "The British Aesthete, cream of the snobbish earth"—symbolized for Lewis by the "matchbox making, dressmaking, chair-painting game" of the "Fitzroy tinkerers and tasters." This type is represented in *Tarr* (1918), by the figure of Alan Hobson, whom Tarr meets in Paris. Hobson's shabby Harris tweeds and large hat suggest the "Art-touch, the Bloomsbury stain," and Tarr presents Hobson with a lightning character sketch of what he typifies:

> "You wear the livery of a ridiculous set, you are a cunning and sleek domestic. No thought can come out of your head before it has slipped on its uniform. All your instincts are drugged with a malicious languor, an arm, a respectability, invented by a set of old women and mean, cadaverous little boys. . . . You have bought for eight hundred pounds at an aristocratic educational establishment a complete mental outfit, a programme of manners. For four years you trained with other recruits. You are now a perfectly disciplined social unit, with a profound *esprit de corps*. The Cambridge set that you represent is as observed in an average specimen, a cross between a Quaker, a Pederast, and a Chelsea artist. Your Oxford brothers, dating from the Wilde decade, are a stronger body. The Chelsea artists are much less flimsy. The Quakers are powerful rascals. You represent, my Hobson, the dregs

of Anglo-Saxon civilization! There is nothing softer on earth. Your flabby potion is a mixture of the lees of Liberalism, the poor froth blown off the decadent nineties, the wardrobe-leavings of a vulgar Bohemianism with its head-quarters in Chelsea!

"A breed of mild pervasive cabbages has set up a wide and creeping rot in the West of Europe. They make it indirectly a peril and tribulation for live things to remain in the neighbourhood. You are systematizing and vulgarizing the individual. You are not an individual. You have, I repeat, no right to that hair and that hat. You are trying to have the apple and eat it too. You should be in uniform, and at work, *not* uniformly *out of uniform*, and libelling the Artist by your idleness." (16–17)

Hobson is a pseudo-artist; he enjoys the freedom of the artist's role, but accepts none of the attendant responsibilities; he degrades art by his antics. He is the Cambridge-Bloomsbury aesthete, who looks back to the Art for Art's sake decadence of the Wilde era, yet who masquerades as something more profound. His bought education has turned Hobson into a mouther of "uni-formed" thoughts; reiterating the conventional clichés of the Establishment and perpetuating a no longer meaningful *status quo*, he tends his *passé* "Victorian lilies" and exults in the name of artist. Lewis everywhere asserts the seriousness of art, and to see wealthy "bourgeois bohemians" playing at art infuriated him beyond measure.

Roger Fry and Clive Bell together symbolize for Lewis the perversion of serious standards in English art. In *The Caliph's Design* (1919) Lewis caricatures the Bell-Fry aesthete "purring" and "gushing" at the Significant Form of a "section of greenish wall-paper and his beautiful shabby brown trousers hanging from a nail beneath it." Lewis draws a basic distinction between those who imitate the forms found in life (usually, he implies, for their jejune "prettiness"), and those who *create* form from the flux, from the chaos of life. The Bell-Fry aesthete is merely representing chaos, whereas the truly creative artist struggles against the flux, imposing a form upon the sprawl of life. But such considerations are beyond the "English variety of art man," as he is caricatured by Lewis:

One artist you will see sitting ecstatic on his chair and gazing at a lily, at a portion of the wallpaper, stained and attractive, on the

89

wall of his delightfully fortuitous room. He is enraptured by all the witty accidents that life, any life brings to him. He sits before these phenomena in ecstatic contemplation. . . . About everything he sees he will gush, in a timorous lisp. He is enraptured at the quality of the country print found on the lodging-house wall; at the beauty of cheap china ornaments; a stupid chair, obviously made for a stupid person; a staring, mean, pretentious little seaside villa. When with anybody, he will titter or blink or faintly giggle when his attention is drawn to such a queerly seductive object. . . . The most frequently used epithet will be "jolly" for the beautiful; and its pursuit will invariably be described as "fun."

Life gushes over the Fry-Bell man who, suggests Lewis, laps it all up with spontaneous, indiscriminate glee. Lewis pursues Fry beyond burlesque into reality, and quotes a passage from an *Athenaeum* article which could almost be a continuation of Lewis's parody:

Objects of the most despised periods, or objects saturated for the ordinary man with the most vulgar and repulsive associations, may be grist to his (the artist's) mill. And so it happened that while the man of culture and the connoisseur firmly believed that art ended with the brothers Adam, Mr. Walter Sickert *was already getting hold of stuffed birds and wax flowers just for his own queer game of tones and colours*. And now the collector and the art-dealer will be knocking at Mr. Sickert's door to buy the treasures at twenty times the price the artist paid for them. *Perhaps there are already young artists who are getting excited about the tiles in the refreshment room at South Kensington.* . . .

Fry is no doubt pursuing a serious thesis here—he is concerned with the relationship of "vulgarity" to art, and the place of fashion in such an equation—but Lewis brilliantly extrapolates Fry's argument to reveal the assumptions lying behind his overt statements. Rather than diagnosing the fashionable, Lewis suggests, Fry *is* merely fashionable; his predilection for kitsch being just that. An aesthetic "honey-bee" flitting from experience to experience without involvement, Fry narcissistically uses art to reflect his own brilliance. The relativist position that Lewis reads into Fry's aesthetic, whereby major emphasis is placed upon the perceiver's subjective experience, (rather than upon the object that the mind approaches), is, for Lewis, a definition of dilettantism:

it denies values enduring in particular works of art, and relegates judgements of value to a modish game dependent upon prevailing intellectual fashions.

One such fashion that Lewis attributed largely to Bell-Fry influence was the current vogue of aesthetic francophilia. Clive Bell's article "Wilcoxism" appeared in *The Athenaeum* on March 5, 1920, and scornfully pointed out the "silliness" of the belief that modern English painting was a rival of modern French painting. The "disagreeable truth," writes Bell, is that "the best painter in England is unlikely to be better than a first-rate man in the French second-class"—critics who assert otherwise "merely make them (the painters) look silly." Bell ends with a few damning words of faint praise for Lewis, before cutting him down with cavalier abandon:

> Let us admire, for instance, the admirable, though somewhat negative, qualities in the work of Mr. Lewis—the absence of vulgarity and false sentiment, the sobriety of colour, the painstaking search for design—without forgetting in the Salon d'Automne or the Salon des Indépendants a picture by him would neither merit nor obtain from the most generous critic more than a passing word of perfunctory encouragement.

Dr. Walter Michel has recently pointed to the Bell-Fry strategy of criticizing British painters whom they disliked: Fry, who "held the most prestigious positions in the art field," pointedly ignored them, while Bell, "whose association with Fry lent weight to whatever he said," consistently denigrated their work.

Lewis replied to Bell the following week in *The Athenaeum*. His letter, full of controlled irony, denounces "the comic Mr. Bell's" French "flunkeyism," and declares him to be "one of the most ridiculous figures we possess." As ever, Lewis's criticism is not concerned solely with ideas, and Fry's character also comes under attack:

> It must be admitted at once, however, that beneath his parade of dishonesty and effrontery, Mr. Bell is really a sincere, if hallucinated, soul. For he regards Paris with something of the awe-struck glee and relish of a professional urchin at the sight of a Cockney guttersnipe. Is there anything that almost any artist with a little prestige in Paris might not tell him that he would not swallow

unhesitatingly? He is almost, you might say deliberately, the comic "Anglais" of French caricature. He is a grinning, effusive and rather servile Islander, out on his adventures among French intelligences.

Lewis had a long-standing antipathy to many aspects of French culture, and one of the first "Blasts" was against "sentimental Gallic Gush, Sensationalism, Fussiness, Parisian Parochialism." To see Bell deliberately ignoring English art and, as Lewis thought, indiscriminately applauding the French, was doubly galling. The first chance Lewis had of replying at length to the Bell-Fry position came in April 1921 with the appearance of *The Tyro*, his "long announced publication."

Lewis's editorial declares that a new epoch is upon us, but the old, not wishing to die, has still a stranglehold upon the present. *The Tyro* represents an attempt to cut free from the moribund past and forge a new aesthetic relevant to the modern movement in European art. Lewis's longest article in this issue is entitled "Roger Fry's Role of Continental Mediator," in which he argues that it would be advantageous for English art to lose its insularity, but, by virtue of his great influence, Fry is the medium of communication between England and the Continent, and his predilections render him totally unsuitable for this role:

> One of the anomalies in the more experimental section of English painting, is that a small group of people which is of almost purely eminent Victorian origin, saturated with William Morris's prettiness and fervour, "Art for Art's sake," late Victorianism, the direct descendants of Victorian England—I refer to the Bloomsbury painters—are those who are apt to act most as mediators between people working here and the Continent, especially Paris. And Paris gets most of its notions on the subject of English painting through this medium. (*The Tyro* I, 3)

All the defects of the moribund tradition come together in the figure of Roger Fry, and in attempting to destroy the myth of Fry's charisma, Lewis feels he is clearing the way for the "New Epoch." Although no single doctrine informs all the contributions to *The Tyro* there is a discernible unity of tone in both the polemics and the imaginative writing. The tone is all that Bloomsbury is not: in place of vague Romantic "prettiness," there is rational, classical astringency; hand in hand with the *Blast*-like iconoclasm, goes the desire to create new positives.

Perhaps the most famous pronouncement of Bell-Fry aesthetics, "Significant Form," is attacked by O. R. Drey in *The Tyro*. In an article entitled "Emotional Aesthetics," Drey takes to task "that well-known publicist and connoisseur, Mr. Roger Fry," for his insistence upon the exclusive importance of formal elements in a picture. Fry's "pleasant little fiction" deliberately ignores the fact that much art patently *has* a subject, and to concentrate solely upon formal qualities is to blinker oneself unnecessarily. As if to provide substance for this argument, Lewis produces his visual Tyros: great, grinning parodies of humanity, like grotesque puppets inexpertly clad in flesh and bone, which leer into the world of reality from the world of art. These figures, which the critic of *The Times* saw as "expletives rather than expressions," thrust themselves into the foreground, denying, by their very existence, the exclusive importance of "Significant Form." As well as being a satire of contemporary habits and a comment upon the human physique, the Tyros are visual propaganda against a redundant aesthetic. In an interview printed in *The Daily Express* (April 11, 1921), Lewis described his new species in this way:

> A tyro is a new type of human animal like Harlequin or Punchinello—a new and sufficiently elastic form or "mould" into which one can translate the satirical observations that are from time to time awakened by one's race. . . . At present my Tyros are philosophic generalizations, and so impersonal. Is this a new departure in art? No, not quite, you must remember that Hogarth didn't die so long ago.
>
> Art today needs waking up. I am sick of these so-called modern artists amiably browsing about and playing art for art's sake. What I want is to bring back art into touch with life—but . . . it won't be the way of the academician.

Satire demands of the reader or spectator that he make a connection between the "fictional world" of the satirical attack, and the "real world" of the subject of that attack. In other words, satire represents the world of art commenting upon the world of reality—and this is as true of Lewis's visual satire as of *The Apes of God*. Thus the Tyro drawings are one method of demonstrating the falsity of the criteria of Significant Form and Art for Art's Sake, which Lewis saw as attempts to elevate art into an aesthetic realm totally divorced from the real world. They are the fruits of Lewis's furious engagement, "blasting tools in hand, upon that granite frontier of the universe of pure form."

Although *The Apes of God* was not published until 1930, Lewis began writing it soon after his Tyro period. Bloomsbury looms large, and is analysed, alongside Mayfair and Chelsea, as a socio-intellectual phenomenon. *The Apes of God* assaults Bloomsbury in two distinct ways: firstly, by means of knockabout farce and personal satire, with recognizable individuals as victims; secondly, by means of "the broadcast," Lewis introduces into the novel a wholly serious conceptual analysis of the significance of this "select and snobbish club." The personal satire is far-ranging; from the sexual ambiguity of Matthew Plunkett, which is reminiscent of Strachey's famous predicament, to the acceptance of Dan Boleyn as a genius (which strongly suggests the "invention" of Duncan Grant by Bloomsbury). Lewis disguised his puppets enough to escape libel suits, but not too much to hinder identification; yet the value of the novel is not as a *roman à clef*, the "apes" are merely symptomatic of a wider *malaise* and it is this which Lewis explores in the "broadcasts":

> It is to what I have called the Apes of God that I am drawing your attention—*those prosperous mountebanks who alternately imitate and mock at and traduce those figures they at once admire and hate.* . . . For a very long time this sort of *societification* of art has been in progress. It is even possible that the English were the first in the field with the *Ape* art-type. The notorious *amateurism* of the anglo-saxon mind makes this doubly likely. In *Bloomsbury* it takes the form of a select and snobbish club. Its foundation-members consisted of monied middleclass descendants of victorian literary splendour. Where they approximate to the citizens of this new cosmopolitan Bohemia is in their substitution of money for talent as a qualification for membership. Private means is the almost invariable rule. In their discouragement of too much unconservative originality they are very strong. The tone of "society" (of a spurious donnish social elegance) prevails among them. Where they have always *differed* has been in their *all* without exception being Apes of God. That is the first point. All are "geniuses," before whose creations the other members of the Club in an invariable ritual, must swoon with appreciation. . . . They yield to none, however . . . in their organized hatred of *living* "genius." Even they have made a sort of cult of the *amateur*—the child artist—and in short any

imperfectly equipped person. . . . But altogether too many Apes and wealthy "intelligentsia" have come on the scene for them to have maintained their unique position. I think you can disregard them. *Bloomsbury* is really only what is called "old Bloomsbury," which is very moribund—the bloom is gone. (131–132)

Although Bloomsbury "no longer had that power to *suppress* that it used to possess," according to Roy Campbell (Lewis's self-styled "literary bodyguard"), it was not too moribund to attempt an embargo in that section of the reviewing world that it controlled. After the *New Statesman* rejected Campbell's review of *The Apes of God* on the grounds that it was "too favourable to Mr. Wyndham Lewis's book," Lewis and Campbell joined forces to produce the pamphlet "The History of a Rejected Review," which describes the impact of the satire and Bloomsbury's reaction to it:

> A prominent "Bloomsbury" is for instance the literary editor of one of the best-known Sunday papers—and so far *The Apes of God* has not been mentioned in that paper. If that silence is ever broken, it will be broken by a roar or a sneer of hatred, or by a sly Bloomsbury *sniff*. (8)

As Lewis suggests in *The Apes of God*, the late 1920's saw the beginnings of a metamorphosis in the structure of "old Bloomsbury," and by the 1930's this change was pronounced. Strachey and Fry died in the early thirties, and a new generation of Bloomsburies—led by Julian, Quentin and Angelica Bell, and her husband David Garnett—injected new life and new friends into the group. Lewis's interests, however, were principally with the "old Bloomsbury" he knew, and in *Men Without Art* (1934) he attacked the "Queen of Bloomsbury" herself, Virginia Woolf. Lewis argues that Virginia Woolf's criticism aims at creating an intellectual *milieu* in which her own "insignificant" art, and that of her friends, might have an honoured position. In defining and exalting the "feminine principle" (which has nothing to do with physical gender: Henry James's art, Lewis declared, also exists in a "twilit feminine universe—of little direct action, and of no gross substance at all" (149)), Virginia Woolf offers an *apologia* for the "peeping" timidity and insubstantiality of her own creations. She creates a meagre world and calls it "reality"; yet the fault, Lewis asserts, lies not in the nature of existence, but in her own

95

Weltanschauung. Lewis brilliantly parodies "Mr. Bennett and Mrs. Brown," showing how "the orthodox idealist tremulously squares up to the big beefy brute, Bennett," and mocking Virginia Woolf's concept of the "New novelists' " difficulty with Mrs. Brown:

> All were boxed with some Mrs. Brown or other, longing to "bag" the old girl, and yet completely impotent to do so, because no one was there on the spot to show them how, and they could not, poor dears, be expected to do it themselves! Do not complain of *us*, then, she implores her public. Show some pity for such a set of people, born to such a forlorn destiny! You will never get anything out of us except a little good stuff by fits and starts, a sketch or a fragment. (165)

Lewis's own aesthetic is, of course, the antithesis of that implicit in the "eternal feminine principle": he believed that life *could* be firmly grasped and examined by the rational mind. The basis of this attack is that Virginia Woolf elevates idiosyncratic predilections into dogmatic aesthetic principles. As his argument proceeds "Virginia Woolf" more and more becomes a symbolic figure, representing the vacuity inherent in the exclusively "feminine":

> Outside it is terribly *dangerous*—in that great and coarse Without, where all the he-men and he-girls "live dangerously" with a brutal insensibility to all the *risks* that they run, forever in the public places. But this *dangerousness* does, after all, make it all very *thrilling*, when peeped-out at, from the security of the private mind: "and yet to her it was absolutely absorbing: all this, the cabs passing."
>
> Those are the half-lighted places of the mind—in which, quivering with a timid excitement, this sort of intelligence shrinks, thrilled to the marrow, at all the wild goings-on! A little old-maidish, are the Prousts and sub-Prousts I think. And when two old maids—or a company of old maids—shrink and cluster together, they titter in each other's ears and delicately tee-hee, pointing out to each other the red-blood antics of this or that upstanding figure, treading the perilous Without. That was the manner in which the late Lytton Strachey lived—peeping more into the past than into the present, it is true, and it is that of most of those associated with him. And—minus the shrinking and tittering, and with a commendable habit of standing, half-concealed, but alone—it was the way of life of Marcel Proust. (169)

However much Lewis overstates his case—and some of his criticism of Bloomsbury is reminiscent of the propagandist iconoclasm of his *Blast* days—his basic premise is incontrovertible. There is a great divide between Virginia Woolf's world-view and that of Lewis himself (call them Feminine/Masculine, Intuitive/Rational, Romantic/Classical, or whatever), and it is precisely upon the "half-lighted places" that Lewis brings to bear his "Kleig light" of reason and ridicule: the result is what Ezra Pound called "writing akin to hyper-daylight."

Virgina Woolf's attitudes are also used by Lewis in his characterization of Margot in *The Revenge for Love* (1937): they are a touchstone of mawkish unreality, and suggest Margot's immature grasp of what life is all about. She exists in a stage mid-way between illusion and reality, and is forever teetering over into the "protoplasm" of her imagination—a self-willed escape from the harshness of a less amenable reality. Margot reads Virginia Woolf incessantly, and the work of this "self-consecrated Bloomsbury priestess" acts as a catalyst to her escapist reveries, as does that of Ruskin—"A Victorian Greenshirt, who stinks of stained-glass and edelweiss and sweats social-credit." Both Virginia Woolf and Ruskin are seductions away from the reality of the present into some romantic "feminist fairyland," where, in Lewis's view, matters of great import are disregarded for the attempted recreation of a mythical nineteenth-century Golden Age:

> Musing at the open window, as if already under the greenwood tree with her favourite author she (Margot) fancied herself back in Oxford (where she had never set foot) at the don's lunch, by the side of her goddess, Virginia (unseen, but there all the same). . . . And (delicately dipping-in, hovering above the delicious pages, in her imagination) she came upon the verses of Tennyson—the literary lord, the Arthurian poetry-baron—as she had done with a thrill of romantic surprise, when first she had entered this "highbrow" feminist fairyland—purchased for five shillings at the local Smith's. . . . Her lips uttered, with scarcely more than a phantom of sound, the romantic declaration. And the words, so diaphanously winged, passed out into the haunted air . . ."*What poets they were!*" she repeated to herself, in the very words of Virginia Woolf. "What poets they were!" *They* being those splendid Victorian monogamists—flowering, as great-hearted passion flowers, hyper-

petalous and crimson red, upon the spoils of the Anglo-Indies and of the Dark Continent. (230–232)

The stylistic parody of Virginia Woolf's "Great Within" is only interrupted in the final sentence which undercuts the romantic dream by exposing the crude reality beneath.

Virginia Woolf's diary reveals that Lewis's taunts struck home, and she knew, "by reason and instinct," even before reading *Men Without Art*, that "this was an attack." Stephen Spender came to her defence in the columns of *The Spectator*, dismissing Lewis's remarks as "malicious." Lewis's reply, which only added insult to injury, stressed that his remarks about "taking the cow by the horns" referred not to Mrs. Woolf, but the Feminine Principle generally! "I have taken," Virginia Woolf confided to her diary, "the arrow of W.L. to my heart," and, all in all, "the W.L. illness lasted two days." The diary does not record her feelings about Margot.

When Lewis returned from Canada after the war, Old Bloomsbury had changed utterly, and the post-war *Zeitgeist* embodied new enmities. The Bloomsbury attitude still existed, but now the coterie had a different corporate personality. New Bloomsbury continued to be an annoyance to Lewis, but much of the passion had gone from the hostilities. Bloomsbury was no longer the symbol of a hollowness at the heart of English cultural life, but was rather the source of local irritations such as Kenneth Clark's "Bloomsbury view" in *Penguin Modern Painters*, or Raymond Mortimer's crushing review of *America and Cosmic Man* in *The Times Literary Supplement*. According to Ezra Pound, Lewis believed that "the scum on the top of the pond (might) in the long run poison the fishes," and for a long while Lewis specifically identified the "scum" with Old Bloomsbury. Looking back over his career, he saw that the "long conspiracy of silence" that had enveloped much of his work had begun in 1913, when he attempted to "hustle the cultural Britannia" and quarrelled with Bloomsbury. The fight was long and bitter, and Lewis's reputation suffered greatly from the patronizing "Bloomsbury Sniff" that, for many years, constituted the orthodox critical attitude to his work.

5

Satire, Apes and Behaviour

Lewis's reputation evolved from that of the *infant bizarre* (of the *Blast* days), through the "author of *Tarr*" stage, until, in the early twenties, he was increasingly accepted as a "serious" intellectual. Hand in hand with the seriousness of such works as *The Art of Being Ruled*, *The Lion and the Fox*, and *Time and Western Man*, went an iconoclasm which could be both intellectually violent and playful. Lewis's "enemy" *persona* was not limited to his journal of that name, and *One-Way Song* suggests one of the public masks he presented to the world at this time:

> Good fighters
> When-driven-in-corners are common: but here's a fellow
> Who does not wait to be trapped—an aggressive fellow.

The Apes of God, published in 1930 but begun in the early twenties, continues both these Lewisian traits in what was to be the biggest *succès de scandale* of a very controversial career. This monumental satire is "hardly a novel," wrote Lewis, "though people remember the name . . . best" (*Letters*, 273), and Ezra Pound described it as "essential to an understanding of a twenty-year period." *Tarr* was a preliminary sketch for what Pound called this "smashing big canvas of the boil on ole England's neck." In the earlier novel, the *milieu*—the artist-quarter of Paris—is extremely vividly achieved, but is essentially the back-cloth against which the action unfolds. In *The Apes of God*, however, the evocation and analysis of the cultural scene is the *raison d'être* of the novel. In *Rude Assignment* Lewis describes the novel thus: "The social decay of the insanitary trough between the two great wars is its subject, and it is accurate. . . . The extreme decay of the bourgeois era preceding the present socialist one was what I depicted. It was in its last sickly saraband" (199, 200).

The peregrinations of Dan Boleyn (a young "queen" of exceptional beauty) through the drawing-rooms of Bloomsbury and Mayfair form the central section of the novel. Dan is cast in the traditional rôle of the *naif* whose experiences are the medium of the satire, and whose innocence highlights the vices, hypocrisies and stupidity of the satiric victims. But here the convention is given a typically Lewisian twist—Dan is "innocent" to such an extent as to be moronic, and represents one of the principle forms of the pervasive "anti-intellectual campaign" that Lewis anathematized in *The Art of Being Ruled* (1926). The child artist is denounced in that book as "one of the most destructive engines in the war against the conceptual strong-hold of the intellect" (397). Dan conveys a satirical judgement upon certain of the characters, only to be implicated himself in a more comprehensive satiric vision. The only character who is free from attack is Pierpoint. By means of Horace Zagreus, Pierpoint masterminds Dan's entry into society with the intention of having him accepted as a "youthful genius." On his travels, Dan stumbles across the full range of Lewis's *bêtes noires*: Bloomsbury pseudo-artists, sham intellectuals, homosexual poseurs, psychoanalysts, ignorant aristocrats, nymphomaniacs, cunning *nouveaux riches*, sycophantic critics, braggart flagellants, the Irish, Oxford poets, lesbians, socially exclusive coteries, pseudo-Prousts, jazz, militarism, youth cults, primitive cults, genius cults, and many, many more. Lewis is not always general: James Joyce, Roy Campbell, Aldous Huxley, Gertrude Stein, Gide, Cocteau, and many others, both by name and allusion, are implicated in the virulent and incisive attack. This great blast of punitive satire forms the central section of the novel, and it is framed by two sections about Lady Fredigonde, the "ex-gossip-column belle." These form a prologue and epilogue to the knockabout satirical farce.

The emblematic opening strikes the keynote of the novel; the image of Lady Fredigonde is superimposed upon the cavorting of the apes like a sardonic *memento mori*. This erstwhile beauty is now grotesque; her machinery of locomotion has become decrepit, and her movements are described in terms of primitive engineering:

The unsteady solid rose a few inches, like the levitation of a narwhal. Seconded by alpenstock and body-servant (holding her humble breath), the escaping half began to move out of the deep vent. It abstracted itself slowly. Something imperfectly inanimate had cast off from a portion of its self. It was departing, with a grim paralytic toddle, elsewhere. The pocket of the enormous chair yawned just short of her hindparts. It was a sort of shell that had been according to some natural law, suddenly vacated by its animal. . . . They passed out of the bedchamber door in their dead-march time—the dark coadjuvant in awful step, skull bowed, with the countenance of a pallbearer. And then (black as a Spade-queen) the pall itself as it were, the dolmen, the catafalque, advanced on end, in a dreadful erectness. (28)

The odour of death is everywhere, yet Fredigonde drags around her misshapen, just-vital corpse with myopic pride. Lewis, like a true Cartesian, is here laughing at the ugliness of the body in decline, and the ridiculous way in which Fredigonde still preens herself merely heightens the sense of the grotesque:

He had seen the lipstick's trail at close quarters, he had smelt the breath blowing straight out of the no-man's land of death at the hollow heart of the decrepit body. (35)

Lady Fredigonde reappears in the final chapter of the novel which is set in 1926, the year of the General Strike in England. Lewis fuses the idea of the strike—metaphorically, a seizing-up of the body politic—with a literal physical seizure, and Fredigonde dies, imagining herself a "bride of love" for the homosexual Zagreus. The conclusion of the novel is an example of what Eliseo Vivas has called "a constitutive symbol," which is a symbol "whose referend cannot be fully exhausted by explication, because that to which it refers is symbolized not only through it but in it." Through the imagery of the grotesque Lewis seeks to redefine the *Zeitgeist* and to revalue the "gay twenties."

There are obviously two types of satirical attack being made in *The Apes of God*: the first is the sarcastic reduction of certain recognizable individuals (or coteries) to what Lewis sees as their proper size. Secondly, by means of Lady Fredigonde, Lewis comments, not upon the follies and vices of individuals, but upon qualities inherent in life itself. The main butts of the personal satire are the Finnian-Shaws, the closely-knit family of poetasters, at whose country home a party takes place which is one of the focal points of the novel. In 1930 the Finnian-Shaws were immediately recognizable, and if there is now any doubt as to their identity a letter from Lewis to T. S. Eliot is revealing:

> In *Lord Osmond's Lenten Party* the name Stillwell (if too suggestive of certain people) could be anything you like— "Bloomsbury" could be deleted . . . I even think that in any case another name, for the purposes of the extract, had better be given to Lord Osmond. (*Letters*, 141)

A protracted guessing-game was carried on in the social columns of the English newspapers as to the originals of the "apes." Montague Slater writing in *The Daily Telegraph* mentions Osbert Sitwell's anger, and states that "Aldous Huxley and Norman Douglas have armed themselves with whips and scorpions." Roy Campbell proudly claimed to have sat for Zulu Bates, a hearty profligate, and there are many similarities between James Joyce and Jimjulius Ratner, the second-rate writer with the "epiphany" style, whose "ambition led him to burgle all the books of western romance to steal their heroes' expensive outfits for his musty shop" (154). Richard Wyndham, Sydney Schiff, Edwin Muir, Lytton Strachey and Bloomsbury *passim*, were all mentioned in connection with the novel. It was with no little satisfaction that Lewis wrote to Richard Aldington: "The agony column of the *Times* has echoed the rage of people who considered themselves attacked in the Apes" (*Letters*, 190).

As an attack against "Sitwellism" and allied socio-artistic coteries, most critics saw the same fault in *The Apes*: "You are inevitably reminded," wrote Slater, "of the God Thor using his invincible hammer to crack monkey nuts." Lewis countered this type of criticism by claiming that satire is not to be judged by the status of the "victims" and, writing in *Men Without Art* four years later, he pertinently invokes *The Dunciad*:

> Against Pope and against Swift, this charge has specially been brought—that the persons they assailed were small. Cibber, Budgell, and Settle, unworthy of notice were such people! . . . But the splendour of the persons involved—the moral status, or the magnificent intellectual presence—is scarcely a measure of the

importance of a work of art. I have seen pictures of peasants (to turn to the plastic arts), and even of idiots, that were certainly greater pictures than other ones of more imposing persons depicting emperors or princesses. (149)

Lewis portrays the Sitwells as wealthy buffoons, extravagantly fawning upon editors of poetry anthologies and interminably reminiscing about mawkish childhood experiences. But the castigation of his personal antipathies is not an end in itself. Looking beyond the furore caused by the outcries of the satirically wounded, Ezra Pound stressed a literary reading rather than a biographical one: "In eighty years no one will care a kuss whether Mr. X, Y or Z of the book was 'taken from' Messrs. Puffin, Gruffin or Mungo. The colossal masks will remain with the fixed grins of colossi" (*The New Review*, Jan. 1931, 54). The Finnian-Shaws/Sitwells are not important *per se*, but are part of a metaphorical statement, valid even if one is ignorant of those satirized. If *The Apes of God* is to be more than a historical curiosity, then the satiric fiction must be able to stand independent of its "social interest," and it does—Lewis has painted the portrait of a society in decay, and as such *The Apes of God* transcends the merely contemporary and personal interest of who's who.

Lady Fredigonde is not "taken from" anyone—the two sections forming the "death framework" are pure satiric fiction which is aimed, not away from the reader (towards the Sitwells and other butts), but towards the reader: in laughing at Fredigonde we are laughing at ourselves. Lewis's abhorrence of the exaltation of purely physical life and his disgust with bodily functions are very reminiscent of Swift in their intensity. In *Men Without Art*, Lewis affirmed that "human life had better, here and now, and once and for all, be accepted as a very bad business indeed . . . it is only a matter of degree between us and the victim of locomotor-ataxi or St. Vitus's dance" (263). The reader is not allowed to miss Lewis's point about Lady Fredigonde: it is just conceivable that these sections could be read as farce or burlesque; if this is so, Lewis reorients the reader by pointing to the universal implications of the portrait:

> None of us are able in fact, in the matter of quite naked truth, to support that magnifying glass, focused upon us, any more than

the best complexion could support such examination. . . . *Every individual without exception is in that sense objectively unbearable.* (270)

This non-fictional interpolation is Lewis's means of controlling the reader's response; it achieves the same end as the omniscient narrator in, say, *Tom Jones* or *Middlemarch*. E. M. Forster has diagnosed the disappearance of the narrator in modern fiction as being due to the sophisticated reader's dislike of the "bar-parlour chattiness" of the author's voice. In *Tarr*, Lewis used the protagonist as a *persona*, embodying many of his own ideas in his conversation and actions. In *The Apes of God*, however, he uses impersonal statements (called "broadcasts") to underline, stress and elucidate elements of his fictional world. These broadcasts are an infallible touchstone to judge the validity of statements and actions in the novel. They are, in fact, Lewis's voice filtered through Pierpoint and through Zagreus, but still pure Lewis.

There are several well-defined levels of awareness in the novel. Lowest of the low is the "youthful genius," Dan Boleyn, who is even more ludicrous than the main butts of the punitive satire, the Finnian-Shaws. Zagreus is above them, Blackshirt comments upon Zagreus and, above all, reigning supreme, invincible, untouchable, unseen, is Pierpoint. As if putting into practice *The Code of a Herdsman*, he never appears in the novel and exists in a different world from that of the apes; he is above the flux of social/animal life, issuing absolute statements from a stronghold of Olympian calm. His existence in the novel asserts that there are other worlds and other values beyond those of the apes. He is the apotheosis of the outsider, who can stand back and see things as they really are—"one of the only people who see." In the novel Pierpoint functions as disembodied mind: Tarr was always embarrassed by his body and its needs—Pierpoint is Tarr without such physical handicaps. He is both pageant master and chorus: "I will make (the apes) parade before you in their borrowed plumes like mannequins, spouting their trite tags, and you shall judge if my account is true" (131). He sits in the wings, observing, commenting, and attempting to make sense of the chaos—but is powerless to change anything, since to act in the pageant would mean abdicating the role of outsider. Again, like so many of the ideas in *The Apes of God*, this could almost be a fictionalization of one of the central concepts of *The Art of Being Ruled*:

> The intellect is more removed from the crowd than is anything: but it is not a snobbish withdrawal, but a going aside for the purposes of work, of work not without its utility for the crowd. . . . More than the prophet or religious teacher, (the leader) represents . . . the great unworldly element in the world, and that is the guarantee of his usefulness. . . . And he should be relieved of the futile competition in all sorts of minor fields, so that his purest faculties could be free for the major tasks of intelligent creation. (432)

Pierpoint's status in the novel, and the relationship with Zagreus, his mouthpiece, also dramatize an important Platonic concept. Just as Tarr/Kreisler dramatize the Cartesian dichotomy of intellect/emotion, so Pierpoint/Zagreus represent the dualism between the perfection of the word and the limitation of the deed. Perfection is only possible in the mind of the philosopher or the artist; once there is movement from the realm of ideas, and there is introduced an element of human action, any notion of the ideal must be dismissed. As Lewis wrote in one of the *Rotting Hill* stories, "My Disciple": "All the dilemmas of the creative mind seeking to function socially centre upon the nature of action; upon the necessity of crude action, of calling in the barbarian to build a civilization" (257). When Zagreus holds the stage at first, he appears to be, in his own words, "Pierpoint's Plato"—but all his words of wisdom are "broadcasts," and as soon as he becomes himself he is just another ape: " '. . . isn't he the worst ape of the lot?' " asked Blackshirt. " 'Does he not take all his ideas from Pierpoint? Is he not essentially a rich dilettante?' " (252). Pierpoint is the only truly creative mind in the novel; the others, believing themselves geniuses, are merely imitators. They ape the artist who, as maker, is God. "Whenever we get a good thing," wrote Lewis in *The Art of Being Ruled*, "its shadow comes with it, its *ape* and familiar" (219). Blackshirt is nearer the ideal than anyone else, simply because, through discipline, he has negated his own personality and attempts to approximate his idea of perfection. He is an ape—but his god, the novel asserts, is a truer one.

For Lewis, fiction was forever pulling in opposite directions: either away from reality into pure fantasy (e.g., *The Human Age*), or away from an imaginatively created universe to actual events in the contemporary world (as in his non-fiction short stories in *Rotting Hill*). The "broadcasts" in *The Apes* point the reader away from the fictional world towards the everyday world, and the effect of these reality-interpolations may be compared to the use of newsreel in an imaginative film: the juxtaposition of real and fictional creates an ambiguous plane of unreality which modifies our response both to "fact" and fiction—we are forced to look at the cavortings of the apes in the light of Pierpoint-Lewis's intellectual standards:

> I have laid bare for you the present predicament of art. I have given an outline of the present dispositions of its natural audience —showing how the decline in their wealth, culture and sense of responsibility has brought down with it those intellectual activities that depended upon it . . . I am not a judge but a party. All I can claim is that my cause is not an idle one—that I appeal less to passion than to reason. (133)

The oracular broadcasts cover three main areas: ideas about satire, the relationship between "truth" and fiction, and the reason for the decline in aesthetic standards. The first of these declarations of aesthetic policy comes in discussion with Lionel Kein, the "pseudo-Proust":

> How is it that no one ever sees *himself* in the public mirror—in official Fiction. . . . Everyone gazes into the public mirror. No one sees himself! What is the use of a mirror if it reflects a world always without the principal person—the Me? Let us put it in this way. You would not like to look into such a mirror and suddenly find *yourself* there. (267)

This statement is very Swiftean, and the image of the mirror is also used by Swift in The Preface to *The Battle of the Books*:

> Satire is a sort of glass, where beholders do generally discover everybody's face but their own; which is the chief reason for that kind of reception it meets in the world, and that so very few are offended by it.

The ideas are identical: satire has become debased and, instead of being virulently anti-establishment, it is now part of the establishment of bourgeois art. Lewis again follows Swift in formulating a solution to revivify pusillanimous satire: it must be made more cruel and the victims should be made to feel its lash. The language in which these premises are expressed is also similar. The first is from *The Apes*, the second from *A Tale of a Tub*:

> It would seem that it is impossible to devise anything sufficiently cruel for the rhinoceros hide grown by a civilized man and a civilized woman. (268)
> . . . there is not, through all nature, another so callous and insensitive a member as the World's posteriors, whether you apply the toe or the birch. . . . Satire being levelled at all is never resented for an offence by any. (The Preface)

When considering these affinities in satiric theory, it is important to remember one of Lewis's early "blesses": "Bless Swift for his solemn bleak wisdom of laughter." This solemn laughter is antithetical to the "simple laughter" of humour: it is the satirical laugh which, as Zagreus says, contains "the harsh metallic bark that kills." It is the mirthless, sardonic laugh of the intellect, occasioned by what is true rather than what is comic. This is the laughter caused by Fredigonde and the black, inhuman vision of the death-in-life framework of *The Apes of God*. The novel suggests its own exegesis, and the broadcasts forever prod the reader towards a deeper understanding of why he is laughing, and what his laughter implies.

The second part of the broadcast goes on to explore the relationship of art to objective reality: "The world created by Art—Fiction, Drama, Poetry, etc.—must be sufficiently removed from the real world so that no character from the one could under any circumstances enter the other (the situation imagined by Pirandello), without the anomaly being apparent at once" (279). This aesthetic criterion is most obviously seen to be fulfilled in Lewis's painting: his "geometrical art" being an attempt to bring stasis to the flux, to tame life and capture the form beneath the flesh. At first sight *The Apes of God* seems antithetical to this principle: the sprawling formlessness of the novel appears to be an impressionistic rendering of the formlessness of life, and not at all "creating gentle order in place of natural chaos." However, as Lewis himself stressed in *Rude Assignment*, the novel does adhere to his "two worlds" aesthetic: "It is not portraiture. A new world is created from the shoddy material of everyday, and nothing does, or could go over into that as it appeared in nature" (199). The extravagant grotesqueries of *The Apes of God* are, indeed, nearer Ben Jonson's characters of humours than anything in "the real world"—closer to a Gerald Scarfe sketch than a photograph—but as an absolute statement about fiction, this principle must be seen in a wider context. One of the major aesthetic evils brought about by the merging of the real world with the fictional world is, according to Lewis, the reduction of the novel to "a dramatized social news-sheet." Proust—"for years the gossip-column writer upon the staff of the Figaro"—is specifically mentioned as "one of the high priests of gossip," who do not create, but merely "edit" their material. "What is called fiction is in large part the private publicity machinery of the ruling society," and it is, or is not, successful according to the cleverness with which the writer has shuffled around his disguised "personalities"—it panders to an exclusive clique who know who's who, and who can say: " 'What an objectional bore (or cad) So and So is! I think the author's much too kind to him. . . . What an old bore that Lady X must be! How could people possibly go to her dreary Lion-hunting parties?' " (277).

The other major theme in these critical interpolations is concerned with the lowering of aesthetic standards (to "Lyon's level") in every facet of contemporary popular culture: " 'The film-play of post-war is the homologue, upon the mental plane, of the War "gasper," from the standpoint of palate. And the thrillers of Edgar Wallace also are a sort of "gaspers." Mental "gaspers" ' " (421). There is a general *exposé* of the perverted and untalented literary world, from the "litero-criminal circles of New York" to the "sex oddities" (like Gide) of France. Gide's *The Counterfeiters* (1925) is the *roman à clef* in this literary decadence: written by a homosexual about an author with homosexual tendencies, the plot concerns the clandestine activities of a group of child criminals. It even has "social interest" (in Lewis's derogatory sense), in that Duchamps, Cocteau, and Alfred Jarry are all "in it." These, and other asides in this broadcast, have the effect of throwing the mind outwards—away from twenties London, to similar art-worlds of America and France, suggesting that this novel is a paradigm for the state of Art in the modern world. As Lewis wrote in *Men Without Art*: "Art will die, perhaps. It can, however, before doing so, paint us a picture of what life looks like without art. That will be, of course, a satiric picture" (225). This is, in fact, the picture we have in *The Apes of God*.

Lewis's next two novels, *Snooty Baronet* (1932) and *The Roaring Queen* (1936), both touch upon aspects of the "insanitary trough" not encompassed by his earlier novel. But in comparison with that encyclopedic satire, they are lighter works: parts being more interesting than the whole. A rambling, cosmopolitan picaresque, *Snooty Baronet* is a first-person account of a rogue's travels from London to Persia via the Camargue. Unlike *The Apes of God*, however, the *picaro*'s adventures are not held together by a formal framework or a single-minded satirical intent. Structured around Snooty's journeys, the novel begins and ends *in medias res*.

"Snooty Baronet" is the journalistic epithet used of Sir Michael Kell-Imrie, behaviourist, writer, and one-legged man of the world. On his return from New York, he is pestered by his literary agent, Humphrey Cooper Carter (Humph of the Dickensian "Chin"), and his leech-like, dithyrambic mistress, "Old Val." Humph decides for Snooty that he should travel to Persia to investigate the primitive Mithras cult for a new book. Acquiescing, Snooty hopes that Val and Humph will take to each other, thus ridding himself of two tedious relationships. The party stops off in the Carmargue where Snooty plans to pick up his pal, Rob McPhail, the all-action, bullfighting poet of gossip-column fame. It is as a model of impassivity that Snooty watches Rob gored to death in an absurd bullfight. Undeterred, they travel on to Persia where Humph has decided to have Snooty captured by tame bandits—thus providing excellent publicity for the forthcoming book. In the fracas of the mock-attack, Snooty cold-bloodedly and with great satisfaction— glee, almost—shoots Humph in the back. Having been well looked after by the bandits, he eventually leaves Val suffering from smallpox and makes his way home to a tumultuous welcome. The "lost baronet's" book is published by The Book of the Month Club and is, with all the publicity, a great success.

The most thorough-going satirical attack in *Snooty Baronet* is the presentation of Snooty's behaviourism. Pointing to Professor Watson as his master, Snooty's own brand of behavioural psychology is a *reductio ad absurdum* which puts all humanity on par with an animated dummy in a shop window. Because the behaviourist is concerned *solely* with observable realities, when faced with a well-made dummy he cannot but accept its "reality." Snooty is part of a crowd watching the movements of this advertising puppet:

> There was something *absolute* in this distinction, recognized by everybody there excepting myself. I alone did not see it. What essentially was the difference however? The situation was exactly the same, was it not, as that of the animals in their cages at the Zoo. The other animals (who catch them and keep them there) walking about outside the cages, gazing at them talking and laughing at them—that was us over against the puppet. How surprisingly small is the difference between a mandril and a man! Certainly—but still slenderer was the difference between this stiffly-bowing so-called automaton, and my literary agent, for example.
>
> Obviously the mandril was a far more complex machine than was this Hatter's automaton, and men were still more complex than the mandril. But this automaton *looked*, was dressed and behaved itself, far more like a man than did a mandril. And that word *looked*, that was for me *everything*. (160–161)

Lewis's own comedy of human defamation in, say, the Lady Fredigonde sections of *The Apes of God*, exploits this equation; yet his "method of the external approach" always stresses that the "things" are also "persons"—it is this very paradox, indeed, which is comic. Snooty, on the other hand, with the full authority of Professor Watson's "scientific" backing, denies this. There is more than a little self-parody in Snooty's attitudes, for they are, in one sense, an extrapolation of Lewis's own.

Snooty's judging everything in terms of "behaviour" is reminiscent of Tarr's "indifferent" view of life. Relationships are reduced to the conjunction—or, if prolonged, the wearying attrition—of carapaces with masks. Genuineness is a concept alien to the behaviourist for whom appearance *is* reality. From this point of view Laura McPhail does not react well to the death of her husband:

"It is because I like a bit of straight-forward *Behavior*," admits Snooty, but "certainly from the standpoint of *Behavior* Laura was not behaving at all well, but deliberately obstructing her reflexes. She allowed stimulus after stimulus to pass without response. She had put down shutters against the stimulating assaults of Fate." (220)

Just as Fredigonde is the justification of the stream of consciousness technique—a method, Lewis wrote, "only appropriate to the depiction of children, morons and the extremely infirm"—so, too, is Snooty the justification of behaviourism. "If it is mad to be a *Behaviorist*," says Snooty, "then certainly I am as mad as a hatter." The novel leads the reader to accept the validity of both premises. Snooty's consanguinity with the automaton is made more obvious by his "nickel nether limb, fitted with clockwork," and a mechanically operated Tyro-esque grin: "I slyly ordered out my entire garrison of teeth, out of the black trap where they stood all day in rows, and contributed my little bit of ornament to the scene" (258).

Even though Snooty is the butt of the satire upon behaviourism, like all *picaros*, his actions are also *sympathique*. His attitude to Val, for instance, like Tarr's to Bertha, is too comic to be condemned. Detesting this siren "domiciled in his blood-stream," his desire to escape from her clutches is matched by hers to get him in "The Bed." Undercutting Snooty's aversion, however, is the inescapable wild body urge, and the tension between sexual drive and personal dislike gives rise to a sexual satire that is typically Lewisian. Where Tarr—with Neo-classical astringency—rebelled intellectually against the romantic slush in which he was being engulfed, Snooty's reaction is more physically emetic. The build-up to "The Bed" scene is a controlled exercise in irony:

"Come Valley!" I muttered cordially. She grappled with me at once, before the words were well out of my mouth, with the self-conscious gusto of a Chatterly-taught expert. But as I spoke I went to meet her—as I started my mechanical leg giving out an ominous creak (I had omitted to oil it, like watches and clocks these things require lubrication). I seized her stiffly around the body. All of her still passably lissom person—on the slight side—gave. It was the human willow, more or less. It fled into the hard argument of my muscular pressures. Her waist broke off and vanished into me as

111

I took her over in waspish segments, an upper and nether. The bosoms and head settled like a trio of hefty birds upon the upper slopes of my militant trunk: a headless nautilus on the other hand settled upon my middle, and attacked my hams with its horrid tentacles—I could feel the monster of the slimy submarine-bottoms grinding away beneath, headless and ravenous.

"Oh Listerine!" I sighed, as I compressed the bellows of her rib-box, squeezing it in and out—it crushed up to a quite handy compass—expanding, and then expelling her bad breath. (45–46)

This "Chelsea Enchantress, *Model* 1930," although in need of a Listerine mouthwash, is "behaving"—as a sexual machine— quite adequately. Aware of the inevitable response to imminent stimuli, Snooty tersely tells Val, "Put the pail outside," and waits for her to help remove his leg:

No very long time at all had elapsed certainly, when the folding doors once more came violently open, pulled from the inside on this occasion. A one-legged man hopped out. He was as naked as God ushered him into the world and as the Grave will take him back. Sitting down upon the end of the settee, and bending over the gilt-flowered slop-vessel, this man proceeded to be ill. For the best part of a further quarter of an hour he continued to be ill. (47–48)

Like Dan Boleyn, Snooty is both butt *and* medium of the satire, and his simplistic S-R view (which is comic in itself), also reveals the absurdity inherent in other characters and situations.

Hovering on the fringes of the literary world, Val is "an unimportant humble hanger-on of the big Chelsea 'Party'-bosses and mandarins of the high-brow racket for the rich" (33). Her social aspirations are less pathetic than ridiculous, and her itch to scribble results in long, scandalous, autobiographical novels about the men she has "got in The Bed." Her infatuation with "the world of fantastic nobodies only a rung or two up from herself" is relentlessly mocked. Her mailing list for holiday postcards suggests the socio-literary ambience to which she aspires—it is a whole stratum lower than that to which the apes belong:

This Armada of sunlit messages was destined for London, England. The names upon it, if alphabetically listed, would have afforded a preliminary "Who's Who" of the minor *Gossip Column*

Class—a "Who's Who" of the *Second Class* of the "Gossip" galaxy
—those definitely not Top Drawer yet with a place *somewhere* in
the social Tallboys so to speak—not initiates, but with a right to
an *honourable mention*, but not mentioned yet (except once by
accident)—those who *gossiped* but were not *gossiped of*—a gallery
of the postulants, outsiders *technically* within the Metropolitan
Gossip Area but not of the Gossip World—ex-Stars, impecunious
poachers and brazen gate-crashers—hangers-on and dogs that are
definitely *under*. (167)

Very much part of this coterie world, Humph represents its
attitude to literature. Books and authors are a product to be
marketed; the P.R. of literature have nothing to do with books,
and everything to do with publicity; sales and column-inches are
the criteria of success: this is the reasoning behind Humph's plan
to have his author kidnapped. The projected book around which
Humph weaves so many involved schemes turns out to be, in fact,
the "unorthodox treatise" which the reader has in front of him.
According to Snooty, this book is no novel but a "fictionist essay
on Behavior," and quite often the writer (i.e. Snooty), in Tristram
Shandy manner, directly addresses the reader. The author-reader
relationship is convivial and chatty, and remarkably well-
sustained by means of a racy, parenthetical style. Snooty's
colloquial tone modulates with a mannered and flexible *oratio
obliqua* as inventive and violent as anything in the Lewis *oeuvre*:

> Humph's irrepressible telephone burst out again into a breathless
> alarum, with the spasm of a teething ten-monther. Raging, Humph
> jackintheboxed off his chair, wild-eyed he flew (upon his sturdy
> scampering stumps out-of-sight) to quiet it—to soothe it or to
> throttle it. He hissed into it, ordering it to stop summoning him in
> that uncalled-for way in season and out of season. (85)

Snooty is a "personal appearance artist" and the novel, as if a
protracted dramatic monologue, is *his* creation. In this sense the
novel *in toto* is a parody of the "real-life-drama," cult-of-action
genre which often become best sellers. Bearing in mind that
Lewis's *Snooty Baronet* sold well under 3,000 copies, it is with
nice irony that Kell-Imrie writes of *his Snooty Baronet*:

> The *Book of the Month Club* have taken up these papers,
> entitling them (about this there will be a lawsuit or two) "SNOOTY
> BARONET," which secures for my "human document"—my fictionist

essay on BEHAVIOR—a sale of a hundred thousand copies as a minimum. The *Book Society*, the english imitation of the american affair, also has given me the prize. Both these events (artistically discreditable as they may be) promise wads of ill-gotten dough to the author of these pages. (307)

One of the recurrent themes of Lewis's early writing has already been described as the conflict between the one and the many. In this novel, Lewis uses *Moby Dick* as an archetype of this struggle, and Snooty's response to Melville's tale suggests his own deeply held antagonism towards the mass of humanity. Although Snooty was originally drawn towards the novel because of his affinity with Ahab—"the patron saint, in our English Letters, of the one-legged"—he found himself identifying increasingly with the whale:

I saw Captain A. as the spear-head of the Herd. He stood for Numbers. It was *he*, in fact, who was the giant! As I saw it, it was the great solitary floating colossus that was the private soul, of any creature. Wherever met, that was, in whatever universe, the One against the Many. And it occurred to me that I might do worse than this: To—on behalf of that great lonely wandering animal, but really in the interests of that great principle—to seek to reverse the position, to the best of my powers. I was *another* Ahab, but of an opposite sign.

I thought over this for some months. What I suppose I was doing was to hatch a plot against Mankind, a plot that had only one plotter: for I rapidly discovered that I was alone, with my hard vision, and there was no one alive I could trust. But I kept my own counsel. I never opened my mouth. Returning to the earth (I, like that great amphibian, could only drag myself from spot to spot, I had been wounded, I had been unlimbed) I might hunt down the fool hunters, one by one—lying in wait for them in unexpected places—picking off a few at least. Their only strength lies in their great numbers. I would never attack, upon that point I was firmly decided, any man I could respect, for he would be in the same case as myself. Even if he were bad and treacherous, I would not raise my hand against him. I would mark down and pursue, selected for the purpose, members of those ape-like congeries—gangs, sets, ant-armies, forces of Lilliput, number-brave coteries, militant sheep-clans—fraternities, rotaries and crews. (63–64)

As a militant enemy of all that opposes the principle of individuality, Humph takes up arms against Mankind—a noun

heavy with Lewisian value-judgments—and is a Machiavel for
what he sees as the forces of light. This mock-heroic "enemy"
stance, to which Snooty demonically adheres, provides the motivation behind many of the farcical events of the novel. Like Ahab,
Humph and Val close in upon Snooty; they are symbols of
constriction: the one planning his life to keep him in "The Bed,"
the other to keep him in the headlines: "They desired me to
become their automaton! I would in the end become their
Frankenstein" (153). Within the Chaplinesque comedy there is a
plea for the inviolability of the free spirit; the right of large
mammals to go in peace. In the light of Snooty's idiosyncratic
morality, the imagery of the chase—Val and Humph are always
"hunting" for Snooty—provides the rationale behind his own
"lone-beast" violence. Surrounded, the large mammal either
lashes out wildly or, like Snooty, uses cunning to flee the nets:

> My eyes shone as I heard I was being hunted. I went to sleep
> that night inventing man-traps for my hunters, to catch them in
> next day. One big spectacular trap for Humph. On the whole I
> resented Humph most. . . . But I slept well—I knew that I was
> being hunted, but I knew how it would end—so I was at peace.
> (265–266)

The motivation, the reasoning, the act; all are valid and causally
linked in a coherent manner—good behaviour, in fact. But the
symbolic triumph of the One over the Many is, in its realization,
so bizarre that it cannot be taken seriously. The whole affair—
indeed, the whole novel—is extremely witty intellectual "play."

In the person of Rob McPhail—a thinly disguised caricature of
Lewis's friend Roy Campbell—the cult of action is further
satirized. McPhail's showy penchant for violence reaches a typically
Lewisian end when he is mortally gored by one of Nature's
"horned representatives." The bullfight is ludicrous because so
totally unnecessary, and Snooty's terse comment—"like a football
scrum in a Marx Brothers pantomime"—places it exactly. A
comment in *Men Without Art* catches the tone of Kreisleriana in
the mindless cult of Action for Action's Sake. Lewis is describing
the *ethos* of a contemporary's novels: they "scarcely contain a
figure who is not in some way futile, clownlike, passive, and above
all *purposeless*. His world of men and women (*in violent action*,

certainly) is completely empty of will. His puppets are leaves, *very violently* blown hither and thither; drugged or at least deeply intoxicated phantoms of a sort of matter-of-fact shell shock." These are the dumb oxen of Hemingway's novels. Snooty's own "indifference" is, on the other hand, "perfectly good behavior . . . absolutely routine Watson." As well as being an ideal "Tester," Snooty is also an ideal (and totally absurd) behavioural specimen.

While researching into the Mithras legend, Snooty reads *Sol Invictus—Bull Unsexed* by "D. H. Lawrence." The two pages quoted in the novel are nearer burlesque than parody: *Sol Invictus* stands in the same relation to Lawrence as does the "Gargantuan mental stutter" to Gertrude Stein.

> Mithras got all hot and clammy about the Bull. So as he was so much in love with the Bull, when God ordered him to go in pursuit of it with a view to killing it, since it had broken jail and gone off on its own again (like the wild animal it of course was) he sat down and wept unrestrainedly in the opening of his cave— because he did not wish to kill the Bull at all, seeing that he loved it, passionately.
>
> "Oh why must I kill Bullie-Woolie!" Thus spake Zarathustra. (92)

Here, Lewis's satirical technique depends not upon imitation, but rather upon the extrapolation of one particular trait which, when taken to absurd lengths, reduces the original to a gross caricature of that one facet. Thus, *Sol Invictus* burlesques the "arty voodoo-ism" explored by Lewis in *Paleface*: the "Lawrence" which emerges is a romantic sentimentalist, a dreamer of "invalid dreams" who goes "smelling around" primitive, exotic cults.

The literary satire in *Snooty Baronet* is, however, incidental, but in *The Roaring Queen* Lewis returned to the machinations of the ape-world of art, exposing and ridiculing the power of certain "big-name" reviewers. *The Roaring Queen* now reads like an appendix to *The Apes of God*, as if Lewis felt, on afterthought, that he needed to blast the incestuous "puffing" of those Grub Street critics ever on the lookout for the next "genius." The main satiric victim is Samuel Shodbutt, "self-made Potentate of the Pen," who is a broad caricature of Arnold Bennett—a Lewisian enemy of long standing. The action revolves around Shodbutt at a country-house party attended by the various sized cogs of the

literary reputation machine. Fearing libel action, Cape withdrew
the book before publication in 1936.

The novel opens with "S.S." and his wife leaving Paddington
by train for the Wellesley-Crooks' country-house in Bummenden.
Also heading for the party is Ossie Potter, crime novel *aficionado*.
Ossie's friend, private inquiry agent Charlie Dolphin, warns Ossie
that his "advanced Bovaryisme" is a dangerous trait. Ossie is "too
susceptible to the printed word" and, as would the heroes of his
favourite detective yarns, he takes his "gat" with him to
Bummenden. S.S. has decided that Donald Butterboy's novel will
receive the prestigious accolade of his famous "Book of the Week"
nomination. Ossie, whose own manuscript has been spurned, is
driven by his "Bovaryisme" to murder Donald and implicate S.S.
With all the predictable unlikeliness of a Whitehall farce, Dolphin
turns up to solve the mystery. With pride shaken, S.S. leaves,
swearing never to return.

Just as *Snooty Baronet* parodied the cult-of-action novel of
which it was also an example, so the detective-story interest of
*The Roaring Quee*n reads like a bad parody of Agatha Christie by
Evelyn Waugh. The crime theme, however, is subsidiary, and it is
the Peacockian gathering which is of central importance. There
are many famous names among the *literati* who converge upon
Bummenden: Lilli O'Stein, "great Austro-Tcheck lady novelist
and international log-rolling champion of middle-Europe"; Marcel
Taxi, winner of "The Year's Most Original Book Review," which
was a truly unique review in that it "did not *once* make use of
the word 'genius.' And yet, in spite of that, he conveyed that a
greater writer had never lived." The acclaimed Rhoda Hyman,
winner of "The Cleverest Literary Larceny Prize," talks with the
Secretary of The Biennial Special Award for the Best Homicide, or
the Crime involving Sudden Death (Fiction or Real Life)—called
B.S.A.F.B.H." The star attraction—for this week—is undoubtedly
Donald Butterboy, a Dan Boleyn figure who has just written his
first novel. The blatantly homosexual Donald—the roaring queen
of the title—is engaged to Baby Bucktrout, a sexually precocious
fan of D. H. Lawrence, whose attempts upon the virtue of the
gardener meet with small success.

None of the characters has the statuesque grotesqueness of
the Finnian-Shaws, or the depth of Zagreus, Ratner, Kein and

other apes. The writing, too, is often slapdash, lacking the inventive imagery of Lewis's best prose, and the opening of the novel is one of the few sections which could stand up to Lewis's own "Taxi-Cab Driver Test for Fiction." The description of Shodbutt's train journey is not interior monologue, yet—like Joyce's technique in the Gerty Macdowell episode in *Ulysses*—the tone of the writing defines the character. The grandiloquent rhetorical questions present S.S. as a "bust," a "profile," a "mass," before he is introduced as a person: he is an imposing front; he is, indeed, *all* front. The archaic syntax and inversions strike an ironic note throughout, suggesting the Johnsonian concept that S.S. has of himself. The frequent repetition of his name; the adjectives "almighty," "napoleonic," "imposing," "majestic"; the pathetic fallacy of the locomotive—all contribute to this fine, externalized self-portrait:

Whose was that imposing bust, worthy of Spy (button-holed and adipose-lined from Georgian State banquets) making its lordly way down the Paddington platform? Whose majestic profiled upholstered *embonpoint* was it that blocked for a spell the Pullman corridor—whose hand could it be that had flung the rich travelling rug upon the first class corner seat with that gesture—whose mass that then returned arrogantly to obstruct the corridor?—Whose but Shodbutt's? Who was this but Samuel Shodbutt himself! It could be none other, and there with him almost at his heels was Mrs. S.S.

With appropriate fuss the courteous ten-thirty, panting and with some proud snorts, as of a self-conscious charger (bestrid by a world-beating generalissimo) left the station. At one of its windows, grim and calm, could be discerned the progressive bust (moving on its way with stateliness, conferring lustre upon the entire ten-thirty) of the almighty Shodbutt. Loftily he stared out, and he saw giant posters cravenly soliciting his custom for Craven A, and there was Mr. Drage craftily and kindly eyeing Mr. Everyman, there were the bold brews of Buchanan and Bass, lounge suits of Moss and the glosses of Combinol, the bodies of Daimlers and Dunlop's road-hogging non-skidders—the hotels of the Dee, Don and Spey—the baths of Baden-Baden. And S.S. swept past each and all with napoleonic indifference, in the stately ten-thirty.

Samuel Shodbutt faced the engine and Mrs. S.S. faced the guard's van. As befitted a Lord of Alphabets *en voyage* (we all understand French here? but if not *tant pis*! for we shall be much in Shodbutt's company—it is essential) S.S. sat bolt upright. He was bound for the Oxfordshire borough of Bummenden, and beyond that for the seat of the Wellesley-Crooks—he had his week-end outfit of a fat old dandy in his bulging suit-cases, groaning within the racks. There was his secretary—not a wife, not a money-mate, or a love-mate, but a useful Modern Woman—Joan Salford that was first, now Mrs. S.S. Whereas S.S. weltered cosily and grandly, in the vale of years, Mrs. S.S. was only halfway down her little hill. His third partner. A magnate with a small, sensible non-luxury car, that was S.S. with his latest youngish Old Dutch of a stenographer —business bed-partners, both sleeping, of the flourishing firm of Samuel Shodbutt—S.S. for short—a contented couple. Books *can* be Big Business, they can be that, if properly handled! Books can be the Goods! (7–9)

After this opening, S.S. does not develop but becomes merely a collection of literary vices, and, in fact, the entire *dramatis personae* are as flat as most of the conversations. Like *The Apes of God*, the plot is episodic, but not all the episodes are tied into the overall design. Baby Bucktrout's escapades in the woodshed— with a Tom who defiantly refuses to play Mellors to her Connie— however amusing, seem to belong to a different novel. Like a *picaresque* story without a picaro, there is a diffusion of interest between S.S., Ossie, Donald, and Baby: the result is a loose, baggy monster which comes to life but rarely.

As satire, Lewis's attack concentrates upon Shodbutt's weekly reputation-mongering and the autocratic power of this "Literary Emperor." The identification of S.S. as Arnold Bennett (who was known affectionately as A.B.) is unmistakable. Lewis dated the "Bennett boycott" of his work to the early twenties, and believed that the antipathy between them had cost him dear. "This John Keats would have had much more porridge," he wrote in *Blasting and Bombardiering*, "if this particular Hitler had not taken a dislike to the cut of his hair."

For a number of years Arnold Bennett was a kind of book-dictator. Every week in the pages of the *Standard*, he "dictated" what the Public should read. And more or less the Public obeyed. He was the Hitler of the book-racket. The book-trade said that he could make a book overnight. If he praised it on Thursday evening, by the week-end it was selling like hot cakes. And he became inordinately proud of this accomplishment. He loved power in the way that a "captain of industry" loves power. . . . He "made" one (book) a week. (94)

In 1927, Lewis himself crossed swords with Bennett in the columns of the *Evening Standard* after a hostile review of *The Enemy*. The feud was renewed five years later in *Time and Tide* when Lewis attacked Bennett's "tipster technique" of criticism which led to a "critical dictatorship of the Anglo-Saxon world." This role forced Bennett—in order to hold on to his power—into "repeating incessantly these triumphs." Lewis saw Bennett as the father of what he called "puff and blurb in place of criticism," and in *Rude Assignment* he described him as the "Star salesman for the publishers, and the godfather of as fine a brood of third-rate 'masterpieces' as you could hope to find anywhere." (148)

The Roaring Queen attacks Shodbutt on just these grounds, and in the long ape-conversations, he damns himself, as it were, out of his own mouth. Having emerged from the northern darkness of Snekkheaton-over-Pegpot, S.S. has become the kingpin in the puff and blurb machine: "Shodbutt could ring the bells and blow the trumpets—indeed was it not really Shodbutt who was *Fame?* Shodbutt was Destiny! Shodbutt was Time's Whirligig! Shodbutt was its heart" (96). Shodbutt, also, never reads the books he puffs: a man of his intellectual sensitivity, he asserts, need only glance at the final page in order to "sense genius." S.S. describes to his wife how he decided upon Butterboy's novel for *The Book of the Week*—only an extended quotation suggests the cumulative effect of these bombastic inanities:

"It was the last line that decided me. It carried me off my feet." "Mine too!"
"The last line. On the last page. I said *This is the goods*. And I'm not often wrong. I could tell it at a glance."
"There was one in the middle. . . ."
"I remember! It went deeply—*a line only*. Marvellous. I never read the middle of a book . . . I never read more than the last page. Balzac said he knew what a book was like without even opening it. I can't say that—that's more than I can claim—I take off my hat to Balzac! He was a *genius*! No. I have to *open* them. It's no use—I admit it, I have to open them. But I never need to go farther than the last page. . . . If that doesn't stir me I just shut

it up with a bang, and mark it N.G. But give me the last page—and I'm infallible. Infallible."

"You would be infallible even if you never opened. . . ."

"No. No. Balzac—*Balzac*! Not me! I take off my hat to Balzac! I must *open* it!"

"You do yourself an injustice."

"No. I can't tell if a book has genius unless I open it. No Joanie—not without opening it."

"But Sam, darling, often you *haven't*. It has been sufficient for me to *tell* you, in a nutshell. . . ."

"That is true. Nutshell. Yes!"

"It is perfectly marvellous the way *the slightest hint*—why one word sometimes is enough. I have known you to decide upon the title alone."

"That is true, yes. There have been times. I have often done that. A title—I *have* done it with only the title. But that's risky, Joanie! Risky!"

"I think your flair is unbelievable! I am positive that if you told Balzac the little I have sometimes told you, he could never have been able to judge unerringly—to judge as you have always done. Not even Flaubert could!"

"Ah *Flaubert*! I take off my hat to Flaubert! Flaubert was a genius! He would have told at once—even if the book had never been written."

"I believe he could! But so could you—you know you could. . . ."
(98–100)

Such scenes are intended to foster the impression that the fashionable literary life of England is a farce created by fools for the enjoyment of idiots. Lewis was obviously annoyed by Cape's decision to withdraw the book. Feeling that the Shodbutt machine was mangling his novel, he drafted out a letter to a director of Jonathan Cape which stated, in no uncertain terms, that he had been badly treated. Lewis could have been forgiven had he seen the dead hand of Bennett giving a last-minute thumbs-down to *The Roaring Queen* just before publication. "Such a book," he wrote to G. W. Howard of Cape's, "going to the 'fiction critic' for review, could not be expected to meet with a very cordial reception: the popular libraries could not be expected to coo over it": so it follows, implies Lewis, that "such a book" is suppressed.

6

False Bottoms

At the same time as Lewis was defending *The Roaring Queen* against one publisher, he was reading proofs of *The Revenge for Love*, which was "about to be contemptuously flung upon the market" by another (*Letters*, 242). The novel which Lewis, in the same letter, called "probably the best complete work of fiction I have written," eventually appeared in May 1937—ten months after the beginning of the Spanish Civil War. This was a time when many young English intellectuals, disgusted by the government's policy of non-intervention, were passionately committed to the "cause" of Spain. There was a British battalion in the International Brigade, and many, though not members of the Communist Party, saw Spain as an emotive symbol. Julian Bell, Christopher Caudwell, John Cornford were all killed in action, and the latter's poem, "Full Moon at Tierz," catches the "thirties attitude" held by many of the intelligentsia:

> Here, too, in Spain
> Our fight's not won till the workers of all the world
> Stand by our guard on Huesca's plain
> Swear that our dead fought not in vain,
> Raise the red flag triumphantly
> For Communism and for liberty.

As *Left Wings Over Europe* reveals, Lewis held antithetical views and, in *Rude Assignment*, he assesses the effect of these on the reception of *The Revenge of Love*:

> For the trouble about this book is politics. It has a communist for a hero. No great harm in that. But this is not the dewy-eyed daydream of the parlour-pink imagination, but a tough ordinary little party-man, dialectically primed to do his stuff. It is not

beautiful mushy stuff, but hard practical militant business, he goes through with like a plumber: only a plumber who has to deceive the householder sometimes: has to sabotage perhaps the bourgeois drainage system. In his activities there is a strain of Groucho Marx. All reality sooner or later has a strain of that. . . .

Is this novel pro-communist? Is it anti-communist?—An inevitable question. But when the novelist sits down to write he does not listen to the harsh impunities of *Pro* and of *Anti*. The biologist looks at life dispassionately: if what he discovers is unpleasant, he does not prettify his report. The novelist is, in part, a biologist. (215)

Although there is a degree of disingenuousness here—the novel is as profoundly anti-communist as all Lewis's work—the realization of his attitudes in the novel is not as simplistic as some critics have attempted to argue. The satirical attack in the novel is aimed at the middle-class intellectual's flirtation with Marxist ideology without considering what the application of such ideas would entail. Lewis presents this as a modish game—what Tom Wolfe has called "radical chic"—as much a part of fashion as of politics. Rather than a political novel, *The Revenge for Love* is a novel *about* political commitment, and it was as such that Lewis hoped it would be read. It was perhaps inevitable, though, that in 1937 it should have been judged (and condemned) on extra-literary grounds:

"Some day," he wrote in *Rude Assignment*, "when the passions of the present time are no more than feverish memories, people will take it up and read it as *a novel*—not glare at it with an eye inflamed by politics, which prevents proper focusing and makes the eye see something which is not there at all." (215)

The novel opens with Percy Hardcaster, one of the "brass hats of the class war," arguing a point of existential ethics with his guard in a Spanish prison. Percy has been caught carrying dynamite—not his, he "wields the pen" rather than the pistol— yet, in spite of his guilt and because of his nationality, he is well treated in prison. Aided by a bribed guard, Percy attempts to escape. The scheme, however, is discovered; his accomplice is killed, and Percy is wounded in the leg. In the prison hospital he is again well treated by a nursing order of nuns, and he gradually recovers after his leg amputation.

The scene shifts to England: the next five sections introduce the characters who will eventually come together at the party given in honour of Percy's triumphal return. Victor Stamp is a struggling artist, impecunious and disheartened by his inability to paint a great picture. Margot, his mistress, dotes on him. Tired by "Red bores" and politics, they are undecided about the invitation they receive. However, after talking to Tristram Phipps, an artist friend who is also a communist, they decide to go. Jack Cruze, Tristy's accountant, who perpetually and indiscriminately lusts after a "bit of skirt," fixes his attention upon Tristy's wife, "Gillian Communist."

At the party, Percy is enthroned upon red cushions, on a red settee, surrounded by "Red men and Red women." He creates atrocity stories about his experiences in Spain, and his audience are determined to believe his every word. Behind the scenes, communists and capitalists combine and plan to smuggle guns into Spain. Victor is chosen as the innocent dupe who is to lure the police away from the actual consignment of arms. Enamoured of Percy's reputation, Gillian is utterly shocked when he tells her the truth about his prison experience. When he propounds his working-class version of communism (as opposed to her middle-class ideology) she turns to Jack Cruze for help. Gillian Communist and Jack Capitalist join forces to brutally beat Percy; the *coup de grâce* is a vicious kick on the stump of his amputated leg which puts him back in hospital.

Victor joins a "fake masterpiece factory" in Shepherd's Bush; he receives a wage of £4 a week while his spurious Van Goghs sell for £3,000. Just as he is financially exploited in this venture, so too is he exploited by the communists in the smuggling episode. Percy is supposedly in charge, but he is also a pawn in the big-business game and knows nothing of Victor's role as decoy. After an action-packed police chase, Victor and Margot discover that they have risked their lives for a car-load of bricks; they are killed in the mountains while attempting to escape. Percy again ends up in jail.

Like the Fredigonde episodes of *The Apes of God*, the Spanish sections at the beginning and end of this novel act as a framework. Within this structure the many disparate characters introduced in the intervening blocks of narrative gradually come together and are seen to be interwoven in a complex skein of social relation-ships. All have "attitudes" on Spain; yet all—except Percy and, eventually, Victor and Margot—are far removed from the realities of the situation. This locative framework stresses both the physical distance between the countries and also the conceptual distance between the myopic idealism of the "Chelsea Reds" and *les mains sales* of action.

There are many layers of satire in the novel, but the most dominant is the recurrent attack upon the self-willed ignorance of the "parlour pinks." Because of the Spanish prelude, the reader is continually aware of the reality behind these illusions, and every episode which portrays their philosophising is riddled with Sophoclean irony. The scenario of Sean's party, which apotheosizes Percy *couchant* amid red splendour, is a comic emblem of this ubiquitous sham. It brings together many of the *dramatis personae* of the deception:

> A red patriarch, Percy Hardcaster reclined, propped by a plethora of red cushions, upon a wide reddish settee, in Red invalid magnificence. A red punkah should have been there to complete the picture. He was surrounded by men and women—by Red men and Red women. There were four women beside him upon the settee; in the place of honour Gillian Phipps, pressed up against his sick leg, which stuck straight out pointing at the assembly with all the declamatory force of Lord Kitchener's forefinger ("I want *you*") terminating in an ironshod stump, provided by the Lerroux administration. . . .
>
> Before Percy Hardcaster, both upon the floor and upon chairs, was an impressive grouping of salon-Reds—of Oxford and Cambridge "pinks"; a subdued socialist-leaguer; the usual marxist don; the pimpled son of a Privy Councillor (who had *tovarish* painted all over him); a refugee (an equinal headpiece, flanked by two monstrous red wings, which were the sails flung out by his eardrums, and which moved back against his head, as if he had been subjected to a hundred-mile-an-hour wind, in moments of agitation). And there were three sturdy "independents" ("friends of Soviet Russia") from the headquarter-staff of the Book Racket. (145–146)

The *leitmotiv* associated with these "parlour pinks" is in the form of the recurrent rhetorical question: "in the words of the poet:

'why when we see a communist do we feel small!'' " In one sense the novel is written to nail the lie of this romantically naïve distortion.

The wilful gullibility of the fellow-travellers is dramatized in several comic scenes. One such involves Jack Cruze, a more vicious and totally unattractive Dan-Snooty type, who happens upon Tristy and Gillian when they are talking politics with friends. Jack, mistaking the drift of the conversation, thinks they are discussing Russia:

"It's a fact they're none too fond of us British in those parts from all accounts."

"It certainly seems they're *not*!"

"A business pal of mine nearly got put in a slave-gang."

"A slave gang?"

"Yes—they have slaves. He went nosing round a bit—sort of souvenir-hunting; and the next thing he knew he found himself locked up with two or three dozen other chaps—a proper lot of hobos—in a cell about ten foot by twenty. Or thirty."

"Twenty probably."

"Yes—you're right, it was twenty."

"Was he tied with ropes to other people?" asked Toland.

"I don't think he was tied up. He said the stench was enough to turn you up."

"You bet it was."

"They took his passport away—he never saw that again. And all his money too."

"Was that in Valencia?" Toland inquired.

"No, that wasn't it," Jack said. "What do they call it now? Petrograd. Yes, that's right! Petrograd. He said *the pauperism*—it had to be seen to be believed!"

Noticing blankness—a sort of amazed petrifaction—come into the face of Toland, he hastened to add:

"But there are some classes there it seems who are quite well off with cars and servants!"

"Really?" Gillian said, who had not been listening.

"That was only the folks in the streets he meant. He didn't like them because they gave him a raw deal.—But it's not the capital."

Geometrically in the centre of the blankness that had driven all expression from Toland's face a light broke, an intelligent spark appeared. This spread, or crept, with a discreet slowness outwards, until a slight smile—still hemmed in by the stony blankness—

stood out a minute, and faded again, as he glanced at Jill—sitting and flushing, with surprise, beside her stammering protégé. Then he turned his back upon Jack, and joined again in the Hardcaster racket—the name was conversationally held aloft as a cornucopia at the christening of the classic crops.

"Who told you all that stuff, Jack?" asked Jill angrily frowning down at him. "You are an old nitwit to be sure! Can't you see that's all a pack a lies? Someone has been telling you fairy-stories about Russia, Jack." (109–110)

Time after time Lewis catches the tone of that quasi-religious need of ideologists to have their preconceptions confirmed. This urge is presented as an addiction relentlessly exploited by the power-bosses whose propaganda machine constantly pumps out "Red Dope for Leftie School-teachers." To accept such opiates is, suggests Lewis, an act of *mauvaise foi*—an unquestioning assumption of an extrinsic ethic and a concomitant abnegation of personal responsibility—and this is not specifically a political concept, but has its roots in those early "wild minds" driven by *idées fixes* rather than by reason. Margot's innocence sees through the surface sophistication of the Chelsea Reds to their dead, mechanical uniformity. They appear, in fact, as wild bodies:

> They were not so much "human persons," as she described it to herself, as big portentous wax-dolls, mysteriously doped with some impenetrable nonsense, out of a Caligari's drug-cabinet, and wound up with wicked fingers to jerk about in a threatening way—their mouths backfiring every other second, to spit out a manufactured hatred, as their eyeballs moved. (161)

Gillian is the *type* of this suave political "ape." Propounding socialist equality, she is stamped with an indelible social snobbery and bitchiness which she parades as "honesty." Margot rejects Gillian's patronizing attitude about "her class," and this clash is a recurrent theme throughout the novel. The working-class communists, on the other hand, are presented as pragmatic men of action. Like Hoederer in Sartre's *Crime Passionel*, the professionals employ any means to achieve their end—ends which are, often, as unjustifiable as the means. The distinctions between communist and capitalist are deliberately blurred: all "power-bosses" are presented as exploiters, and "political" objectives are interwoven with motives of personal greed. O'Hara and his ilk, gangsters masquerading as freedom fighters, are less hypocritical but no more sympathetic than the "parlour pinks." Percy, the "navvy turned Marxist schoolmaster," puts himself forward as a man without illusions: his is not "*Intourist* Communism" but rather the "Communism of *Barrikadenfodder*." Although he has great pride in his acceptance of "harsh" realities and his ability to "see things *as they are*," he too, in the final analysis, is the dupe of manipulatory forces. Just as Percy points to a deeper level of reality than that of which Gillian is aware, so his "reality" is revealed as being an equally incomplete picture. In terms of the dominant image of the novel, first Gillian's and then Percy's grasp of "things as they are" is seen to be false-bottomed. This conjuring with levels of reality produces an atmosphere of epistemological uncertainty which has implications beyond the theme of political deception in the novel.

Only the solicitude of Boots' Library for the sensibilities of its readers prevented the novel from being entitled *False Bottoms*—an image which is imprinted upon every major event. Margot's discovery of the false panelling in O'Hara's house points to the wider connotations of this scheme of metaphor:

> As she became accustomed to this very large empty apartment, Margot had felt that she was moving about the inside of an immense box. It was a box that had false sides to it and possibly a false bottom: for she was not at all sure that she was not treading upon trapdoors and the masked heads of shafts, as well as leaning against a hollow wall, in a deceptive security. . . .
>
> She could not reach out, to express her misgivings, into the difficult realms of speech, where all these disparities of thinking and acting would fall into place and be plausibly explained: but she was conscious nevertheless of a prodigious *non-sequitur*, at the centre of everything that she saw going on around her—of an immense *false-bottom* underlying every seemingly solid surface upon which it was her lot to tread. (160–162)

The ambiguous nature of phenomenological reality (in addition to intellectual reality) proceeds from an ineluctable meaninglessness inherent in all existence. As false bottom succeeds false bottom, there is *no* solid ground. Percy, too, voices this feeling in terms which suggest Camus's definition of *l'absurde*. Like many of Lewis's characters, Percy looks into the abyss—the ultimate false bottom. Tristy questions him about his beating by Jack and Gillian:

> "Why, you are a different person? What for? What was it for?"
> Percy shrugged his shoulders.
> "For nothing."
> Serafin himself could not have said *nothing* with more feeling for the false bottom underlying the spectacle of this universe, and making a derision of the top—for the nothingness at the heart of the most plausible and pretentious of affirmatives, either as man or as thing. And that his "nothing" meant nothing, just that, not more and not less, but a calm and considered negation, caused Tristy to stop abruptly and look away. (272)

Victor and Margot, of course, plunge into a physical ravine—an ironical punning finale to their false-bottomed career—in what is the most savage cosmic joke of all. Victor's limited awareness always fitted him for the role of victim, but his dour honesty—he is called the "Kipling man"—adds an aura of tragedy to what could have been a merely grotesque end. The alien Spanish environment had suggested to Margot the "nothingness" underlying its spectacle:

> So with growing apprehension she had trod this sullen soil. Here was nothing fast but a false and deceptive surface. Even its touristic blandishments savoured of deceit. She felt that she had engaged upon the crust of something that concealed a bottomless pit, which bristled with uniformed demons, engaged in the rehearsal of a gala Third Degree, to be followed by a slap-up autodafé, for the relaxation of Lucifer. (288)

Just as the novel traces the process of Gillian's political education—by stripping away the layers of unreality which impeded her vision—so does it define a profound change in Margot's world-view. Moving from the naïve, sentimental acceptance of life that her early response to Virginia Woolf's cosy "highbrow feminist fairyland" suggests, Margot gradually accepts a view of life which takes into account the unromantic, the cruel and the absurd. This change is imaged in several specific scenes, of which the most powerful is her confrontation in the café with the dwarf. His vulgar horseplay and grotesque antics are a great shock to

Margot. Selected as the butt of his pathetic crudities, she becomes part of the floor-show. The whole affair is too much for her, and she experiences what Sartre calls *la nausée*—the inability to digest experience by intellectualizing it. Her bible had been *A Room of One's Own*, and her sensibility, shaped by the *ethos* of late nineteenth-century liberalism, had walked delicately over a tightrope without ever glancing below. Confronted by this grotesque symbol of the uncivilized and, more importantly, the uncivilizable, Margot recognizes the limitations of her vision. There is no escapist "room of one's own" away from alien truths: "things as they are" must be faced. Margot's disillusionment is as traumatic as Gillian's:

> There was no use pretending she did not belong to this system of roaring and spluttering bestial life of flesh and blood. And this sub-human creature had been sent there expressly to humiliate her—as a punishment for something, perhaps! (295)

The dual movement of Margot and Gillian—from the darkness of ignorance into the light—has a parallel in Percy's gradual realization of the value of Margot's love for Victor. Sincerity is foreign to Percy and, as if Tarr's "indifference" had been placed at the service of an ideology, his reactions to any situation are manufactured to fit the party line. Having witnessed Margot's selfless attempts to help Victor, when Percy hears of their deaths he at first feigns a response. Yet later, an unobserved emotion does break through; the mask slips and—even though veiled in irony—Percy concedes his humanity:

> Swollen with an affected speechlessness, Percy proceeded to give a sculpturesque impersonation of THE INJURED PARTY. His cell-mates watched him surreptitiously, with an admiration it was out of their power to withhold. Heavily clamped upon his brick-red countenance, held in position by every muscle that responded to Righteous Wrath, was a mask which entirely succeeded the workaday face. It was the mask of THE INJURED PARTY (model for militant agents in distress). Obedient to the best technique of party-training, he sustained it for a considerable time.
> But meanwhile a strained and hollow voice, part of a sham-culture outfit, but tender and halting, as if dismayed at the sound of its own bitter words, was talking in his ears, in a reproachful singsong. It was denouncing him out of the past, where alone now

it was able to articulate; it was singling him out as a man who led people into mortal danger, people who were dear beyond expression to the possessor of the passionate, the artificial, the unreal, yet penetrating voice, and crying to him now to give back, she implored him, the young man, Absolom, whose life he had had in his keeping, and who had somehow, unaccountably, been lost, out of the world and out of Time! He saw a precipice. And the eyes in the mask of THE INJURED PARTY dilated in a spasm of astonished self-pity. And down the front of the mask rolled a sudden tear, which fell upon the dirty floor of the prison. (376–377)

The values postulated by the novel in opposition to the rigidly doctrinaire hard-line of any "Party," are singularly un-Lewisian. Margot, for all her faults, is finally the touchstone in the novel: her love is the only value not found to be "hollow." No political Pierpoint waits in the wings, and the novel ends where it began— in a Spanish prison. The circular plot suggests that another cycle is about to begin: the forces of manipulation have not been destroyed; nothing has changed. Yet the novel, however tentatively, does close on a note of affirmation: the response of individual to individual is all-important, indeed is all there is, in the face of inhuman systems. In Margot's love for Victor and in Percy's grief, lies the slender hope for humanity against the doctrinaire. Small, human positives to pit against the will-to-power and against the void, yet, even after the deaths of Margot and Victor, they remain vague intimations of hope. One must wait until *Self Condemned* (1954), before these values are further explored and weighed against those—more typically Lewisian—values of the mind.

Looking back on the publication of *The Revenge for Love*, Lewis saw that "it was no time to bring out a serious book." In 1937 the "old Ship of State" was hurrying towards the "lip of the maelstrom," he wrote in *Rude Assignment* (214). By the time he published his next novel, *The Vulgar Streak* (1941), the ominous rumblings had evolved into world war. Set in Venice in 1939, the ambience of this book is, in part, created by the disturbing political machinations in Europe. These events are very much in the background, yet are evident enough to suggest that the old Europe and the old certainties are in the process of disintegration. As the novel opens, two young gentlemen talk about art in a civilized and sophisticated manner; theirs, it seems, could be the

Europe of Henry James: "At the end of the Venetian street were the waters of the Grand Canal, graved with the demilunar wavelets of Venetian art." Yet as the conversation proceeds the "maelstrom" becomes evident: Hitler, Chamberlain, Bad Godesberg, Theo Kordt—the "demilunar wavelets" are deceptively calm. The gracious and charming Vincent Penhale, with his "Clark Gable smile," is thought very attractive by April Mallow, an English girl on holiday in Venice with her mother. But, in Vincent's case, too, things are not as they seem. He reveals to his friend, Martin Penny-Smythe, that far from being the genuine representative of the British upper-crust that he appears, he is, in fact, "the son of a workman" who had been "born in the gutter." Vincent's whole personality is a "false bottom." Built around lies, he has created an imaginary *persona*, given it an imaginary background, and proceeded to imbue this figment with life.

Vincent's attitude to April—she is an upper-class scalp to win—disgusts the highly conventional Martin; Vincent's "vulgar streak" is all too obvious. There are some disquieting moments for April when she sees Vincent (by now her lover) in the company of Halvorsen. The latter is "*a common-and-proud-of-it sort*," but Vincent allays her fears by telling her that he keeps up the acquaintance because Halvorsen once saved his life.

The scene shifts to London. The wedding of Vincent and April had been precipitated by her pregnancy, and they now live in a "smart gentleman's residence" attended by a gentleman's gentleman. Maddie Penhale comes to visit the newly-weds; like Vincent, she has managed to escape the class trap through marriage and, also like her brother, she has the cold manner of someone constantly acting a role not at all suited to her nature. Their father has just died, and Vincent—the self-willed exile—returns to the bosom of his family for the funeral. The mother is drunk; the relatives squabble around the coffin; the corpse is without his false teeth. As the rain pours, the clergyman hurries his prayers, and the coffin is lowered into a waterlogged grave. These are the roots Vincent repudiates.

Vincent is outraged when he learns that Maddie is friendly with "clubman" Dougal Tandish—"a rich top-dog out of the second-best top-drawer of our snobbish plutocracy." Ironically, Vincent despises Tandish's aristocratic pose because the latter "has not a drop of blood in his veins that is not grocer-blood, or Birmingham slum-blood." Suspicious that Vincent and Halvorsen are mixed up in counterfeiting, Tandish is murdered by Halvorsen when snooping around the workshop. In the ensuing police investigations the truth about Vincent is splashed all over the newspapers. April is not at all worried about her husband's origins, but when it is revealed that he is implicated in forgery and even murder, she collapses and dies of a haemorrhage. Everything crumbles; and after a melancholy last supper with Martin, Vincent writes some letters and then hangs himself. Attached to his body is the note: "Whoever finds this body may do what he likes with it. *I* don't want it. *Signed*. Its former inhabitant."

The style of *The Vulgar Streak* is markedly different from that of the earlier novels. Gone is that distinctive element of linguistic play which is unmistakably Lewisian. The prose is more obviously functional: less dense in images and complex metaphors, there is little interest in language *per se*. The new style is relaxed, informal, discursive and, as Julian Symons has said, "perfectly suited to the exaggerative nature of Lewis's high comedy." The low-key tone gives to all Lewis's descriptions a strong sense of irony—as if he is continually parodying the form in which he is working. In a manner analogous to a comedian's deadpan delivery, the unemotive reportage heightens this comedy of attitudes:

> The Breakfasting British, upon the morning of Tuesday, September 27, in their Venetian hotel, were glum and excited. The Berlin Broadcast, reaffirming the German ultimatum to the Czechs, had been digested and slept on and wakened up to, and it now over-shadowed their bacon and eggs. It made the hot coffee and greasy milk taste better or worse according to their ages, intelligences, pocket-books—to their degrees of suggestibility, hatred, or tolera-tion of Hitler, love of God, stake-in-the-country, hope in an afterlife, identification of Christianity with Communism, first-hand experience of war, anxiety for the dog-they'd-left-behind-them, knowledge of Italian, fear of mustard gas. One woman mopped her eyes all the time. She had just received a letter informing her that her only son had joined the Fire Brigade. (65)

As in *The Revenge for Love*, the concept of deceit is central to the novel. Vincent makes a living by passing counterfeit currency, and his own life is analogous to this fraud: he passes himself off as something that he is not. Where the earlier novel exposed the sham politics of the class-war, *The Vulgar Streak* explores— through the medium of Vincent's experience—the social snobberies and tensions inherent in British society. Vincent's upward trajectory is, writ large, the socially acceptable means of escaping from the restrictions of working class culture. His life is one long telephone voice—assumed so naturally that he no longer knows which is the reality. Vincent deliberately creates a social mask which is totally different to his personality. He seeks that which Arghol in "The Enemy of the Stars" found so tragically con- stricting—a social self. Arghol described it thus:

> That creature of two-dimensions, clumsily cut out in cardboard by the coarse scissor-work of the short-sighted group-spirit—the social mind—that impudent parasite had foregathered too long with men, borne his name too variously, to be easily abashed much less ousted. Why, he was not sure, even had they been separated surgically, in which self life would have gone out, and in which kept alight. (1932, 40)

In the puppet-nature hierarchy, Vincent's is an unusual case. As a perfect stimulus-response mechanism, he approaches the automaton status of the hatter's dummy in *Snooty Baronet*; but, at the same time, he is also like Tarr in that he is in control of the machine. The continuously generated false-self crushes and usurps "the real Vincent." In the past Vincent had been an actor, and he is frequently described in the novel as playing a role in a manner that is "exaggerated, reminiscent of the footlights." The reader's response to Vincent is ambivalent. When he first appears he seems to be an out and out snob: " 'I consider punning a mark of breeding, don't you? It is the same order of things as snuff taking. . . . The poor are unable to pun' " (14). Yet when the nature of his conspiracy becomes clear, the response is ambiguous.

Throughout the novel runs the suggestion that behind the "gilded portals, dazzling footmen and bemedalled doorkeepers," the stately London scene is shot through with injustice, fraud and corruption:

> "Half the people who *do* pay never have any food—they haven't any money left for that after they've met these inflated rentals, the most ruinous income-tax in the world, and all the rest of it.

They get thinner and thinner. The only fat ones are the ones who slip between the gaps in the net.—If you see a fat man in London to-day, you may be sure he's a rogue." (153)

Just as Halvorsen, that "enemy of society," justifies the currency forgery ("the modern state is based upon organized-legalized-Fraud . . . to counterfeit its fraudulent and oppressively administered currency . . . (is) . . . an act of poetic justice" (213)), so, too, is Vincent's existential fraud justified. In response to the family attitude that " 'you wasn't *born* to talk like wot you do,' " Vincent declares " 'You are a fatalist, Harry. People ought, according to you, to stop upon the spot where they happen to be born. That's where we differ. I'm all for changing things, and *myself* to start off with.' " (139).

Believing that he is subverting a rotten but rigid class structure, Vincent is, of course, merely assimilated into it—and his "self" is annihilated in the process. His sense of ontological insecurity is the price he pays for his counterfeit existence: "I am a sham person from head to foot. I feel empty sometimes as if there were nothing inside me . . . *I* am not here." Like a complex game of ontological hide-and-seek, Martin mistakes *persona* for person, and after Vincent's confession sees the truth as unreal:

> But *this* was not Vincent Penhale at all. This man he had before him was an impostor. . . . He resented his impersonation of his friend. . . . In spite of everything, Martin clung to his picture of the gentleman. The picture of his friend as he had always thought of him from the start. He *would* not have this bounder thrust upon him. (85)

Vincent's despairing cry to Maddie: " 'I wish I knew what I was really like!' " crystallizes this false-self/forgery theme; a theme which culminates in Vincent's death. The cryptic note abandoning his corpse embodies his realization that his *persona* was merely a shell, a false encrustation, a fantasy, which, after his experience, can now be distinguished from the real self: "*I* don't want it." When Vincent puts his version of the class conflict to Martin, he speaks with the knowledge he has gained through suffering. His social Houdini stunt has failed, and the novel portrays the futility of such a struggle, serving, as it does, to reinforce the class structure. Realizing the worthlessness of his objectives, Vincent's final *anagnorosis* represents a stoical abandoning of society's values: a position defined and defended by Lewis from the earliest pieces like *The Code of a Herdsman* and *The Enemy of the Stars*, right through to *Self Condemned*.

Just as Vincent created his self, so, indirectly, has he created Maddie. Completely influenced by her brother, she is Vincent's shadow and echo. Her social climbing—lacking the self-awareness of his fraud—is, like an enforced prostitution of the personality, even more debasing. Her modelling is a more passive form of counterfeit, but equally destructive of self. Maddie is married to Dick Morse, a young hack cartoonist who had "people" ("professional instead of labouring"), who had been to Manchester Grammar School ("the Westminster of Manchester"), and whose "accent was therefore quite good." Remembering Vincent's advice, she "seeks every opportunity of conversing with people who are upper class"—hence her association with Tandish. Maddie's naïvety is pathetic: " 'I only saw him,' " she tells Vincent, " 'because I thought his accent was so good,' " and her social progress reflects, *in parvo*, Vincent's own. At the end of the novel, Maddie is still modelling and using her beauty to attract a man. In spite of Vincent's recognition of the hollowness of the pursuit, nothing has changed: the class trap still forces Maddie into this passive fraud.

Lewis's version of working class life is grotesque. The Penhale family are presented as ignorant, crude, narrow-minded and—in their own way—as snobbishly exclusive as the "toffs" they despise. With the money Vincent sends home, his mother buys drink; when Vincent returns for the funeral he recognizes that this is where "two old persons had lived and dreamed their drunken dream of old age." The family feuding at the funeral and the arguments over the corpse's false teeth are like stage-business from one of Joe Orton's comedies. Yet Maddie's vision of this drunken, squalid, petty old-age, moving towards a loveless, helpless death, is a characteristically controlled piece of writing; without a trace of sentimentality, Lewis manages to convey the pity behind the horror:

> From the eastern limits of the Harrow Road it was a long way to Hanwell Cemetery, the principal burial ground for West London, and the hearse, for most of the route, set a smart pace. The rain

came down: Maddie found herself watching it splash upon the bald skull of a road-mender, who stood cap in hand, surreptitiously attempting to count the number of wreaths, as the hearse hurried past him.

. . . A dying horse, lying in a pool of blood at the side of the road, was watched by a group of men. They looked to Maddie as if they had attacked it and were watching it die. There was no truck standing near it. Of course *they* were not responsible for the conditions of the horse! The sight had shocked her into a distortion, into *blaming* somebody. The pathos of the great bloodstained horse—struggling to live, its giant muscles striking out for it, in feeble stampings of the air—had torn away the screens, behind which human death is enacted off-stage, its reality sublimated.

She had an inartistic glimpse of a delirious old man, whose equally aged wife had refused him when he had asked to be taken into bed beside her to be warm when first the great chill descended on him. She saw the old man thereupon, like a dying animal, his teeth chattering, crawl out with a closet-like chamber beside the kitchenette and sink panting upon a rickety camp-bed, to face death alone. (126–7)

It is from this *ethos* that Vincent feels he must escape. Like Joyce's Stephen Dedalus, he is constricted: but, unlike Stephen, he does not withdraw; he plunges *into* the social conflict. Feeling that the only means of escape is through "force or fraud," he begins his *embourgeoisissement,* and is proud that he has "dragged himself out of this inferno" (136). The reader sees, though, that Vincent has merely dragged himself into another.

April Mallow is, in many ways, similar to Margot, the redemptive character in *The Revenge for Love.* Both tend to slip into dream worlds divorced from reality: Margot's dream centres on the "poetic" world of Virginia Woolf; April's romanticism is less literary, but equally distorting. She looks at the war through the *Vogue*-tinted lens of women's magazine sentimentality:

She had fallen into a day-dream upon a theme suggested by the word War. Dressed as a hospital nurse, she looked extremely attractive: and she was dressed as a nurse. To none she was more attractive than to a certain pallid and war-worn man, with a head bloody but unbowed, who was propped upon a nest of pillows in a hospital bed. Not an ordinary hospital, but a beautiful one run by the Duchess of Gloucester or the Duchess of Kent (in that order) in a delightful part of England; yes! not far from her home in Wiltshire, indeed conveniently close. Shocking things were happening up in London, bombs were raining down—the balloon barrage, as that Professor-man had forseen, was entirely useless. But here all was peaceful and orderly . . . brutes as the Germans were they would hardly drop their bombs upon a hospital run by the Duchess of Gloucester (or even of Kent) and so these works of mercy might be performed without rumbustious distractions, by all these beautifully dressed Women of England, who hovered round the beds where the haggard young heroes lay, bringing grapes from the buttery for the more attractive, and often sitting down— between dressing wounds and trimly and smartly accompanying the doctor on his rounds—to have a cup of tea with the patient, who, poor boy, was anything but averse to a bit of female company. (20–21)

April's idyllic vision of Keatsian languor is later contrasted with the reality (in terms of the novel) of hospitals. With "classy humanitarian invective," Victor denounces these "slaughter-houses for the aged poor" called infirmaries, and Maddie's nightmare vision of old age endorses such an attitude. It is this uncaring social system that Vincent, in his own way, attempts to undermine. Yet out of the depths of April's mawkish unreality comes the one thing that Vincent sees is "stronger than class" (221). She represents the same positive human values as did Margot, and, in one sense, this is a new version of the Lewisian formula of the One against the Many.

Running parallel with the theme of acting is the theme of action. Mr. Perl, the psychiatrist, in analysing Vincent's condition, functions as did the broadcasts in *The Apes of God*—his interpretation guides, informs and deepens the reader's response:

"You are an egotist. . . . Let us forget *class*. That is not the whole picture. Whatever station in life you had appeared in, it would have been the same. There is something about you (it is very *interesting*) that is proper to you, and independent of education. It is obvious, Vincent, that you suffer to a morbid degree from . . . an *excess of Will*.

. . . Your will is so powerful that it drives you along like a restless tyrant. You have a sort of *personal dictator* (to parody 'personal devil') inside you . . . Mussolini and Hitler what are they, but extreme, and curiously disagreeable, expressions of this morbid

138

Will. Devils they are not, so much as diabolical machines of empty *will.*" (183)

This idea is later developed in conversation with Martin: just as Julien Sorel was the representative man of the Napoleonic era, so the age of Hitler has produced Vincent. More sophisticated, less Dostoevskyan than Kreisler, he is an embodiment of the *mal du siècle*: the modern will to action. Vincent tells Martin of his belief that " 'all can be achieved by *action.* . . . Europe has run amok. In my little way . . . I have reflected what is biting Europe' " (235).

The Revenge for Love used the form of the political thriller for more serious ends; *The Vulgar Streak*, through the medium of the "social novel," presents reflections on contemporary social and political issues. " 'I have proved,' " says Vincent, " 'upon my little personal stage, that force is barren. Conceived in those hard terms of action-for-action's sake nothing can be achieved, except for too short a period to matter. I have *proved* that, have I not?' " (235). Both novels reveal Lewis experimenting with conventional genres for didactic ends, something he was to pursue—less success-fully—in *Rotting Hill* and *The Red Priest*.

A collection of short stories entitled *The Two Captains*, sub-mitted for publication in the fifties but never released, takes up many of the illusion/reality themes of these novels. The story which gives its title to the collection is a further exploration of the social and individual forgery concept of *The Vulgar Streak*. Captain Murray Mason, a Vincent-type "perfect gentleman," feels strongly that the Central Banks are perpetrating legalized fraud. His attitude to the fiscal system is a development of Halvorsen's: " 'Every time I come in to cash a silly little cheque,' " he tells his friend who works in a bank, " 'I feel the same about those little wads of brand-new notes, smelling of the factory where they forge them all.' " Basing his argument upon the immorality of the Capitalist finance system, Mason persuades his friend to embezzle his employers. This is not a crime, he claims, but rather a " 'spirited action (which takes) from them a small fraction of their pelf.' "

Like Vincent, Mason's financial fraud is both symbol and symptom of his wider fraudulent activity. His occupation as a

139

commercial artist consists in concealing meagre realities behind distorted images: a process, the story shows, that has spread into every facet of his existence. In a typical Lewisian conclusion, where the "twist" in the story is given an extra turn, Murray's social mask is shattered by another, even more devious, mask. However, the finest presentation of the counterfeit theme comes in "Doppelgänger," a story published in *Encounter* in January, 1954. Thaddeus Trunk, famous ageing poet, lives in the mountains of Vermont with Stella, his English wife. Surrounded by acolytes who dote on his words, he plays "the Dispenser of Culture to . . . benighted Mankind." Thaddeus, however, has allowed himself to be transformed into a "publicity-figure"; he has *become* his reputation:

> He wishes to *live* his publicity figure. There it is inside his house —in his bedroom, in his bed, a publicity figure, not a real man. . . . A man's publicity is a caricature of himself; it is really how the public sees "greatness." (24)

The story partakes of mythological reality. The stranger who comes to visit Thad is his *alter ego*: "I have no jingo reputation to keep up, so I can say what I think." Thad is so wrapped up in his Ezraic grand manner that his actions are a pastiche of the real self. This is an archetypal pattern in Lewis's fiction, and his final rendering of the paradigm—set in the mountains of Vermont— has all the atmosphere of a folktale. The story ends with Stella leaving the "Publicity Scarecrow" for the "uninvited guest":

> That was the last Thaddeus saw of his wife. Or, to state briefly what had happened, a second Thaddeus, whom Stella recognised as the real Thaddeus had made his appearance, and Stella, very simply, changed Thaddeuses, deserting, or, if you prefer it, leaving, Thaddeus Number One. Only a shadow, a shell, remained upon the mountain. . . . But, bit by bit, this advertisement figure evaporated, and there was nothing left at all of the one-time poet who had been devoured by that Moloch, the Public. (33)

"The Weeping Man" and "Children of the Great", both from *The Two Captains*, look at different aspects of the person/ *persona* conjunction. The former pursues the wild body theme: under every civilized exterior lurks an atavistic autonomic system. Bob Allen Crumms, however much he wishes to approximate the "masculine ideal," is finally reduced to a bizarre hysterical complex of physiological responses which make a mockery of his mask. In "Children of the Great," Derick Gilchrist, the "obscenely dull" son of a famous American historian, adopts an ignorant pose which, he hopes, everyone will believe is an affected "antic disposition." Concentrating upon the layers of deceit, self-deceit, and counter-deceit in the relationship between Gilchrist and his wife, the story presents complex and subtle variations on the counterfeit theme. Perhaps it was because Lewis was so interested in externals—in what he called "the wisdom of the eye"—that the paradox of seeming and being was so central to his work. Appearances, in one sense, are everything (all else is mere conjecture): yet, on the other hand, appearances are completely ambiguous. From this very ambiguity Lewis created one of the recurrent themes of his fiction.

7

The Horrors of Peace

> Millions of men and women in periods of peace are being killed
> too—slowly poisoned with bad food, starved with inadequate food,
> exposed to disease (where the rich are not), improperly cared for
> when sick, allowed to die like dogs when old, fleeced by insurance
> companies to ensure a proper burial—but I need not enlarge upon
> the horrors of peace. (*America and Cosmic Man*, 214)

Lewis's return from America coincided with the election of a
socialist government in July 1945. The result of the election was,
in the words of King George VI, "a surprise to one and all." The
war had drained Britain's resources; this country had the largest
national debt in the world and everything was in short supply.
Within ten months, bills were before parliament for the nation-
alization of the coal industry, the introduction of National
Insurance and a National Health Service. "We are the masters
now" was the cry of Labour; a new era was dawning. It was,
however, also the era of Cripps's ration "coupongs," prefabs,
spivs, bread rationing, one egg a week, whalemeat and snoek.
A fuel crisis which put two million people out of work was followed
by a currency crisis which lost seven hundred million dollars in a
month.

This is the era Lewis chronicles in *Rotting Hill*: "The stories
in this book are in fact one story, that of a society adrift, like
a shipwrecked crew upon a raft: fifty million people upon a wet
and windy island in the Atlantic ocean." Most of these pieces are
undisguised socio-political tracts, given the name "stories" only
because the ideas are put into the mouths of "characters." The
collection attempts to portray "the rot" in every facet of contemporary life, from the rot in the cloth of the Anglican Church

to the rot in the wood of Lewis's Notting Hill home. For Lewis, the Welfare State is a symbol of the muddled thinking of this "Crippsean ice-age." The impulse to the greatest good for the greatest number has reduced that good to a shoddy "utility" standard. The specific ills Lewis catalogues are legion: in two pages he mentions shirt buttons that do not fit the holes; shoe laces too short to tie bows; jackets of inferior manufacture; a "Strachey loaf" which is inedible; strawberry jam made of carrot pulp; scissors that will not cut; poor quality tea, and a shortage of butter and sugar. The tone of much of this volume is drab and prosaic, conveying—often fortuitously—the drabness of the forties. But all too often the strength of Lewis's feeling is not fictionalized, and the result is a bad-tempered outburst at what now seems a trifle. This is from "Mr. Patricks' Toy Shop":

> From nail-scissors we went on to speak of other symptoms. For instance: replacing the metal screw cap on any tube or bottle was invariably difficult. It stuck, it joggled about: those small daily operations were not accomplished smoothly, there was friction and time wasting. The cause? Badly-finished goods was the only answer. The caps of toothpaste tubes never fit neatly. I waste half a minute every morning coaxing the cap on to mine, that is three and a half minutes a week—say fifteen minutes a month, three hours a year. Ink-bottles which I use a lot are nearly as bad. As popular counter-irritants to the bad bread and flour (there are hundreds of new ones on the market) are other examples of time wasting ill-made metal stoppers and caps. But the instances of careless manufacture are legion. (222–223)

Several pieces have "Wyndham Lewis" as narrator/protagonist, and the best of these—"The Bishop's Fool" and "My Disciple"—combine the form and manner of fiction with adherence to a non-fictional reality. The stories, taken as a collection, never live up to the promise of the parts. The opening of "Time the Tiger," for instance, is as imaginatively dreary as "Mr. Patricks' Toy Shop" is just dreary. The digestion image encompasses the sky; the very fog is suffering from socialist depression; politics, in this dyspeptic age, have infected everything:

> It was, as usual in London about that time of the year, endeavouring to snow. There had been a hard frost for days, in fact it was so cold that in any other country it would have snowed long ago. The

sky was a constipated mass, yellowed by the fog, suspended over a city awaiting the Deluge. It was eight-thirty in the morning. The streets of Rotting Hill were like Pompeii with Vesuvius in cata-strophic eruption, a dull glare, saffronish in colour, providing an unearthly uniformity. The self-centred precipitancy of the bowed pedestrians resembled a procession of fugitives.

Mark Robins was standing at his bathroom window. His eye followed with displeasure the absurdly ominous figures moving under mass-pressure to be there at nine o'clock, passing on through the hollow twilit streets towards the swarming undergrounds. It was the urgency that jarred, their will-to-live as a machine. (163)

A comparison of "The Bishop's Fool" and "My Fellow Traveller to Oxford" highlights Lewis's success and failure in this collection. The former presents Samuel Hartley Rymer (Rev.), a political clergyman who could be one of the "parlour pinks" from *The Revenge for Love*. After a chance meeting in the British Museum, the "overoxfordized" Rymer comes to see Lewis. Their arguments are a means of delineating the parson's utopean socialist idealism— and thus the political theme is central—yet, at the same time, Lewis has created a splendidly bizarre comic character as pro-tagonist of his cautionary tale. Lewis the artist is as much in evidence as Lewis the political journalist. Physically gauche and intellectually left-handed, Rymer is a personification of his ideology; yet there is as much concentration on his idiosyncratic psychology as on his ideas. Under the scrutiny of Lewis's "tough eye," Rymer opens up, "and I looked in, as if into a woman's handbag" (8). Just as Jack Cox physically assaults Rymer, so, Lewis suggests, will actuality assault the idealistic political dream in which the clergyman exists: he cannot, though he would, ignore reality. The comic inflation of overstatement is a stylistic analogue of his intellectual bombast. Lewis weaves fantasies around his naïve yet charming buffoon, while, in the process, taking a swipe at the "liberalism" of the Church of England.

It is the level of imaginative involvement that marks the success of "The Bishop's Fool": the Condition of England debate is fictionalized and embodied in a self-sufficient framework. In "My Fellow Traveller to Oxford," on the other hand, there is very little art concealing ideas. Between Paddington and Oxford, Lewis converses with his fellow traveller (in the political as well as the physical sense) about the hierarchy of social rights. This is a lively enough piece of political journalism, containing some memorable throwaway lines—"the man who barters his liberty for a set of false teeth and a pair of rimless spectacles is a fool"—but it is of more interest to the social historian than the literary critic.

A glance at Lewis's letters during the late forties reveals just how much of *Rotting Hill* is rooted in depressing autobiographical events. Yet, often, these very experiences are transformed into the magnificently malevolent comedy evinced in his best satires. "The Rot" describes the repairs to the dry rot in the Lewis's Notting Hill flat. Physical decay is symbolic of the ubiquitous cancer in society: "one rot is truly involved in another rot. From the epidemic ravaging 'better-class' houses to the decay of the classes for which they were built is a logical transition" (94). To combat this, the landlord sends a cockney carpenter who flings himself "into the tracking of the rot with the avidity of a ferret." The whole affair soon develops into a token class-war, and the workers—playing football in Lewis's living-room, wrecking more than they repair—subtly take revenge upon their erstwhile masters. Not only does Lewis catch the ebullient mood of Labour's "We are the masters now," but he also dramatizes—rather than vents—his own reactions:

> For were they not Dalton's boys? And they were the merriest, noisiest, laziest in this bankrupt land—where "too much money chases too few goods" but what of it? On the Utility level nix is in short supply. We live on Utility level, for ever and ever—what of it? there won't be no other. Hurrah for Utility-life, with money to burn in Austerity Street, at the blooming old pub at the corner. Hurrah! cried the painters as they smoked their Weights, Hurrah! Hurrah! Hurrah! ...
>
> The entire house shuddered with their freedom.
>
> I sat pulverized. There had never been so inconsiderate a fury of undisciplined joy by the upstairs workers. The longer the job dragged on, the more careless they became. But these men were intoxicated with what I still regard as a sacred beverage—liberty. I was ruled by this great liberal scruple. As they scuffled and kicked around overhead, choking with the hysteria of the Harrow Road, gulping with Hammersmith fun, for a ball they used, I imagined, a wad of my old newspapers, tied up in an oil rag. They

had before. Their trampling was atrocious. I put my book away and stood up. The shindy grew in wild intemperance. "Goal," panted the fat painter. *What* goal? (Once you unchain one who has never tasted freedom, his wild ego will know no limit. But I did not desire to be the person to recall these men to order.) I put on my hat and moved silently out, as in certain circumstances, rather than strike a man, one would abruptly make haste to leave a room. (103, 106)

"My Disciple" is another autobiographical piece which casts "Wyndham Lewis," misunderstood philosopher, in the leading role. Mr. Gartsides, an art-teacher in a Bermondsey Elementary school writes to Lewis for advice about policies to follow in his new job as director of a Rochdale college. Gartsides, "the man with the ugly name" who inhabits ugly provincial neighbourhoods, represents the post-war utility art-man. For seventeen years an army sergeant in India, he decided to "go in for" education, and emerged from a one-year emergency scheme as a fully-fledged art teacher. His concepts of spontaneous self-expression are antithetical to Lewis's severe classical ideal, yet, in a *locus classicus* of philosophical misunderstanding, Gartsides takes Lewis as his guru. This "intoxicator of innocents," who has no time for the easel picture, incites his "Giles-like-gnomes" to indulge their predilection for intuitive *graffiti*:

> A thigh thrown over a desk, an arm akimbo, his utility shoe dangling, the children were addressed by Gartsides; and their fidgety little eyes popped out of their curly little heads. They were told that what was *spontaneous* was best. Spontaneous meaning what *spurts* up, free and uncontrolled, not fed out by a nasty *tap*. The freest expression—the most *innocent* release—of their personalities was what *he* was there to teach. They would get no *direction* from him, his role was that of a helpful looker-on. Ready to give a hand, that was all. (He conveyed a very vivid impersonation of these transactions I am obliged naturally to abridge). Art was *doing what they liked*. It was not doing what *he* liked. They must pay no attention to him or to anyone else—it did not matter a hoot what *anyone* thought. He waved a rebellious eye over towards the office of the superintendent. He could teach them nothing. (253)

Although Lewis points out that these ideas are closer to the aesthetics of Herbert Read, Gartsides will not be moved: Lewis's *The Caliph's Design*, he insists, has had more influence upon him

146

than anything else. This comedy of errors embodies one of Lewis's basic philosophical tenets:

> "I had a vision" (Lewis tells Gartsides), "like my Caliph—but suppose for a moment that I had found a social revolutionary . . . to act upon my vision. What would he have done with my vision? Naturally what Hollywood does with a literary masterpiece. He would have diluted, vulgarized and betrayed it. . . . All the dilemmas of the creative mind seeking to function socially centre upon the nature of action; upon the need of crude action, of calling in the barbarian to build a civilization." (257)

In terms of this analysis, Gartsides is the "barbarian" who has made a botch job of *The Caliph's Design*. Ideal and action are inimical; Gartsides is all crude, untutored action; even his pictures, he tells Lewis, are "rotten"—suggesting that his art is symptomatic of this blighted era.

Lewis's successes in *Rotting Hill* are undoubtedly those stories in which he creates convincing characters, but all too often the ideas are uninteresting. During a tedious exposition about the relationship of individual freedom to centralized authority in "Parents and Horses," Lewis points to what must ultimately be seen as the failure of this "non-fiction fiction":

> The quotations will not, I hope, have been found too fatiguing. All this minutiae, if it can be tolerated, provides one with a close-up as it were, which is invaluable for the student but rather irksome to the general reader. I have taken this risk because of the necessity in such a case to provide convincing factual data. (296)

In the light of Norman Mailer's experiments with "the novel as history," it is tempting to see *Rotting Hill* as a species of *Erlebnisdichtung*—perhaps "the short story as reportage." In a style reminiscent of his most lively pamphleteering—say, *The Old Gang and the New Gang* (1933)—Lewis's social commentary is often wildly extravagant and flamboyantly provocative. Flailing out at people as well as institutions, he "blasts" such divergent figures as Stalin ("a Czar in a cloth cap") and Churchill ("a stooge of the Left"). "If my characters are obsessed by politics, it is because today our lives are saturated with them," writes Lewis in the foreword to *Rotting Hill*, and it was just this obsession and

147

saturation that he was to pursue in his final novel, *The Red Priest* (1956).

This novel is firmly rooted in facts of the fifties: it is the era of Mau-Mau atrocities in Kenya, juvenile delinquency, J. B. S. Haldane, Donald Wolfit, the Red Dean and, most centrally, "progressive" Christianity. The "rot" and post-war squalor have grown a little older, sired a new race of diminutive child thugs— their natural habitat the bomb-site, their territory the streets— and an internecine battle between rival gangs forms the prelude to the action of the novel. This is a world grown used to living with the rot: the disease, while not proving fatal has, like septicaemia, poisoned every part. The older generation stands aghast while delinquent mob rule transforms reality into Grand Guignol:

> "Perhaps you remember our Mews is blessed with a bombsite. Our domestic refuse collects there, or a good deal of it. A hideous uproar issues from it, our cans and broken crocks fly across it, smoke rises from the bonfires, composed of what we have discarded. Our private letters are read with storms of cackles, garments we have said goodbye to clothe a fiercely marching Tom Thumb, trailing in the gutter behind. Sometimes an ambulance dashes down the Mews, headed for the bombsite, and speeds away, carrying one or more bleeding midgets—material for the Casualty Ward. A drunk, one night, come from a party at one of the minor legations which swarm in our neighbourhood, lay down and died. Well, the corpse found its way on to our bombsite. A reptilian brat was seen squatting on his chest attempting to light a cigarette he had stuck in the dead mouth. As if it had been picked by vultures, one-eyed, and the grinning head a mass of tiny holes, the dead man was rescued by the police." (16)

Through this squalor glides Augustine Card, the Red Priest; Man-of-Action (and of God), Card is physically impressive and his charisma stuns many who come into contact with him— especially women. The first impressions of this "beautifully dressed, handsome cleric" whose "powerful body was sheathed in a cassock," are gained through the eyes of Jane Greevey, a middle-aged spinster already under his spell. Card is a Christian "progressive" who attempts to synthesize Church and social justice through the medium of political action, and he uses all the vulgar techniques of public relations to advertise his cause. Card's disciples see him as a man of saint-like idealism: his detractors as a cunning, thuggish con-man who has "painted the church red." The reader, initially deceived by Jane's romantic attachment to Card, quickly moves from the former to the latter view.

Like Kreisler, Augustine Card is a critique of the Nietzschean man-of-action. Educated at Eton and Oxford, his civilized sophistication is only a veneer, beneath which exists the violent "Blond Beast." A friend of his at Oxford had described him thus:

> "This Norse giant, this perfect type of a Stone-Age Cave Man was also a Dunce, he took to book learning with difficulty. I discovered him in our rooms at Oxford, struggling over the simplest mathematical problem. It was there that I felt, as I watched him crouched over his books agonised, that I had a man from one of the backward epochs of humanity in my rooms with me. I helped him with the simplest equations, took him, step by lubberly step, through the most childish Latin exercises.
>
> "In his last months at Oxford he advanced fiercely into the realm of Divinity, uttering barbarous cries which horrified me. But for some mysterious reason, he felt at home there! He developed the most horrific theories. I had never felt afraid before, in his company. But when I became a Doctor of Divinity, I was frankly terrified. He locked me up in my room, on one occasion, and kept me locked up for a day until I agreed to praise the beauties of the most horrible heresy. . . . All the life of a fighter is lived in the Stone-Age, or some such epoch. No man of intellect or high intelligence can be a fighting man, simply because in order to be that he has to live a Stone-Age kind of life. To remain supremely an animal is essential for a successful fighter." (150–151)

Card's egomania often confuses publicity for God with self-publicity: he was, according to this same friend, the sort of man "who could kill his grandmother, and willingly go to the gallows, gloating over the columns and photographs in the press."

Staking everything upon "the dynamism of his personality," Card asks for total commitment to his religio-political crusade. He is fired by the conviction that "the Basis of Communism is Christianity," and he brings Russian priests to his church. His analogy between the ideals of the Sermon on the Mount and those of Soviet Russia causes an uproar—ending in a fight. Mary Chillingham falls victim to Card's emotive proselytizing and helps in a crude piece of propaganda during a particularly controversial sermon: leaping to her feet at the first rumblings of discontent from the congregation, she cries " 'I, for one, follow Father Card wherever he leads.' " Mary and Card eventually marry.

Despite Mary's attempts to "civilise (her) Teeny," his excesses continue. He moulds his personality cult as carefully as a pop-star, and his megalomania is highlighted by the continuous jarring of low comedy upon the High Church ambience. On the birth of their first child, Augustine is photographed offering him a glass of champagne, "or putting a wafer saturated in it between the infant's lips." His finances are frittered away by ridiculous stunts which earn his parish the title of "Our London Oberammergau." Because Mary refuses to part with any of her inherited capital, their relationship becomes strained. Card grows more extreme: he employs "bouncers" in church and, finally, plans " 'with a dozen young men, to march with Jesus into Whitehall.' " Augustine's revolutionary-innovatory activities come to an abrupt end when, after a dispute with Makepeace, his curate, there is a fight and the ex-boxing blue kills his assistant.

After serving three years for manslaughter, Card decides to "dedicate (himself) to a religious life of the most repulsive kind." He becomes a missionary among the Eskimos, but there is no escaping his nature. Mary soon receives word that her husband, having killed an Eskimo, has himself been murdered. A second son is born after Augustine's death and Mary names him Zero: "She could see that he would look like his terrible father; that he was fated to blast his way across space and time."

Although the social setting of the fifties is important—in that it gives a context within which Augustine's predilections are fostered—unlike in *Rotting Hill*, this is not the *raison d'être* of the novel. Augustine is a fine grotesque and, as in *The Wild Body* stories, the presentation of his "religious" obsession is of central importance. Augustine is a mass of contradictions: he exhorts his congregation to "think small," for example, yet he himself is diabolically proud. Indeed, after his prison sentence he feels no guilt for his action, only shame that he might be "cut" and blackballed at his club. His maniacal delusions of sanctity are too insane to be classed as hypocrisy, and the brutal fanaticism of the man who " 'held in (his) hand the bomb of Jesus' " is, in spite of the violence, paradoxically innocent. Like Conrad's Lord Jim, Augustine tries to flee from his social disgrace: the choice of the frozen northern wastes is heavy with symbolism—it is, in a sense, the natural home of this throwback to "Neanderthal man." Civilization, however "rotten," has not yet retrogressed to the primitive crudeness of this extremity: here Augustine is in his element. His death—as if savaged by animals, "throat gouged out"—is a fitting end for this Mau-Mau of civilization. Like the canine violence which ends the late story "The Man Who Was Unlucky with Woman," this is a typically Lewisian critique of pure action.

Several familiar Lewisian themes are pursued in *The Red Priest* without being fully integrated into the novel's design. The long section on Hambledon College—which is to education what the Van Gogh factory is to art—seems to exist solely in order to provide Lewis with the opportunity of exposing sham values in education. Hambledon institutionalizes those misplaced yearnings for surface sophistication which bedevilled Vincent in *The Vulgar Streak*. The college director boasts of their achievements:

"Up here we provide people with a short general training, which fits them to some extent for all kinds of vocations. We are in fact phonies, as you no doubt realise. A man here can learn to pretend to know something he doesn't. We are quite efficient in a phoney way, and that does supply a want. The teaching staff are most of them university men, and we *could*, although of course we don't, supply a man with all the necessary information about life in Oxford or Cambridge, and we *could* arrange him to pass himself off as having been at one or other of the universities. We do not connive at these things, you understand, but we do privately think that a number of crooks pass through our hands." (98–99)

This finishing school for phonies—and the protracted discussions about curricula and teaching methods—might have fitted better into *The Vulgar Streak* than this novel, where the "counterfeit" theme is not so fully worked out.

It is as if the prolonged fantasy of *The Human Age* had entirely absorbed Lewis's mythopoeic faculty, and he was unable to fictionalize the day to day reality without, either *in propria*

151

persona or through one of his characters, being overtly didactic. The socio-political comments in *The Red Priest*, the crude archetectonics of the plot—like broadcasts without the flair of *The Apes of God*—give an impression of scissors-and-paste construction. Like the earliest pieces for *The English Review*, the "fiction" and the thesis are too easily divisible; but, unlike the earlier stories, Lewis did not revise his last published novel. These late fictions are the logical extension of Lewis's conviction that art must be "about something"; they represent the final comments of a man who never ceased to believe in the educative effects to be gained from the world being forced to contemplate its own image.

8

The Everything or
Nothing Principle

Self Condemned is Lewis's most impressive work of non-satiric
fiction, and it stands as one of the most powerful tragic novels
of our time. The tripartite structure plots René Harding's
inexorable fall from eminence, through poverty and disparagement, to his symbolic death. René is the last in a long line of
Lewisian "Natures"—men apart, perfectionists among pragmatists
—who, in attempting to live on a "heroic moral plane," find that
they cannot escape all human contingencies. Through the horror
of his own fate, he drags a trapped and unwilling wife whose
destiny is tied to his own as securely as a rock to a suicide's
neck.

René is a forty-seven-year-old Professor of History who resigns
his Chair because he no longer believes in the history he is expected
to teach. Deciding to emigrate, he takes leave of his mother and
three married sisters; they cannot comprehend his reasons any
more than can Hester, his wife. Only Rotter Parkinson, a friend
of long standing, seems to understand; his "article" about René
clarifies the latter's ideas and actions. Conventional history, he
believes, is a mere cataloguing of events perpetrated by power-
politicians no better than gangsters; the important aspects of the
past—the arts, philosophy, scientific discoveries—are merely
relegated to footnotes. René, whose *Short History of World
War II* had been dubbed "fascist" by *The Times*, sees the
imminent war as "crazy and extremely wicked."

In Canada, the Hardings settle in Momaco's Hotel Blundell;
their home is a room twenty-five feet by twelve. Totally ignored
by Canadian intellectuals, they spend three years in this "lethal

chamber." Everything about the "city of the Ten Commandments" appals them. The hotel-life is as brutal as the world outside, and their room becomes a retreat from the horrors of reality; in adversity, man and wife grow closer together than ever before. René accepts these hellish conditions and slips into an intellectual hibernation, but Hester never ceases to think of escape. Cedric Furber, a wealthy book collector, employs René for a few hours a week to help catalogue his library. The manner in which René clings to this sinecure contrasts sharply with his idealistic resignation. This chapter in their lives comes to an abrupt close when fire engulfs the hotel.

The fire destroys the "passionate solidarity" the couple found in their room. As René becomes more accepted by Momaco, Hester becomes more depressed: her need to return to England is as great as his conviction that Canada is the best place for him. Through Furber, René meets Iain McKenzie, a professor of philosophy at Momaco; emerging from hibernation, he again feels the thrill of intellectual activity. Eventually he is offered, and accepts, the Chair of Modern History at Momaco; he does not take seriously his wife's unhappiness and can rationalize her over-emotional reactions. René is called from an academic dinner to Police Headquarters; Hester has thrown herself under a truck. The experience spiritually kills him. Retreating to the isolation of a Catholic seminary, he finally emerges "a glacial shell of a man." The man who accepts, "with a mechanical thrill of frigid delight," the prestigious Chair offered by a North American university, is only a "half-crazed replica of his former self."

The complex moral choices that face René are nicely analysed by Lewis. The first decision to resign is taken without reference to anyone—not even Hester. Such issues must be decided in isolation: anything else is merely truckling to a group spirit. He explains his dilemma to Mary, his sister: in a sense, Hester's happiness is quite irrelevant in this matter:

> "When one thinks these things out for oneself," he began, "that is one thing. It is quite another thing when one begins to share one's thoughts with other people. Complexities make their appearance immediately. I thought this all out for myself without consultation with anybody."
> "You certainly did," Mary agreed. "There is no doubt about that."

"Just as it would be impossible to write *Paradise Lost* or *Hamlet*, collectively, so it is impossible to plan some major change in the individual life, collectively." (22)

Once the decision has been made, René is unshakeable; there can be no alternative: "It is destiny," he tells his sister. This intellectual arrogance is tempered with nobility: his unwavering integrity is grand rather than grandiose:

> "You may ask, cannot I think differently? Why can I not purge myself of this order of thinking? Well, of course there are some things that everyone thinks which hot irons could not burn out of them. It is the circumstances of the time in which we live which have made it impossible for me to mistake my road: there have been signposts or rather lurid beacons all the way along it, leading to only one end, to one conclusion. How anyone, as historically informed as I am, can come to any very different conclusions from my own I find it hard to understand. They must have blind eyes for all the flaming signs." (18)

While writing *Self Condemned*, Lewis described the central theme of his novel in a letter: "As now planned it will be dominated by the 'everything or nothing principle.' This means a character who is what today colloquially is known as a perfectionist. Woman has been called 'the eternal enemy of the absolute'; so our perfectionist must encounter immediate difficulties when he comes in contact with woman" (*Letters*, 410). The conflict between René's will and Hester's "feminine," emotional longing waxes and wanes throughout the novel, René's will always dominant. A fine line divides the "designs of the perfectionist" from the wilful selfishness of the egotist, and Mrs. Harding's query echoes through the book: " 'You are not by any chance a fool, my son?' " This does not shake René from his resolve, yet it does force the reader to reconsider his absolutism of will. The nature of René's decision is stressed from the beginning of the novel; "le roi René" is described with heavy irony:

> Le roi René was not a man to be unconscious of style, in himself or others. He delighted to swim through space with the air of a Louis the Eleventh, bearing himself as a King of France hurrying to meet the Emperor Maximilian. He realized that his gait and gesture were too superb for his status or for the occasion. But this

amused him. Sometimes he would deliberately act the king, or the statesman, about whom he was just then reading. De Richelieu he was very fond of impersonating. . . . (48)

In *The Lion and the Fox*, Lewis quoted A. C. Bradley on the "fundamental tragic trait" of Shakespeare's heroes. They are men worthy of our admiration, "built on the grand scale; and desire, passion or will attains in them a terrible force":

> In almost all we observe a marked onesidedness, a pride of position in some particular direction; a total incapacity, in certain circumstances, of resisting the force which draws in this direction; a fatal tendency to identify the whole being with one interest, object, passion, or habit of mind. (119)

In Bradley's terms, then, René is an archetypal tragic hero: his "fatal flaw" being that very absolutism of will which raises him above group-thinking mankind. At the end of the novel, Lewis states more explicitly that "will-to-success, of the most vulgar type" was René's failing. As in the case of Thaddeus Trunk, who is both great poet and phoney—so, too, is René both "vulgar" egotist *and* heroic figure. Like Faustus, René over-reaches himself; having renounced the "compromise of normal living", he condemns himself to the "heroic moral plane" he has chosen. Rotter's article points to both aspects of this choice:

> "Professor Harding's way of seeing the world is, then, analogous to the Vision of the Saints. But it is not necessarily in any way connected with saintliness. What this system amounts to, in reality, is a taking to its logical conclusion the humane, the tolerant, the fastidious. It is really no more than that with great rigidity and implacability, you pursue these things logically to a point where all that doesn't belong to them or that contradicts them is absolutely repudiated. But René Harding would say, 'Why not take these things to their logical conclusion? what is the use of them indeed, if you do not take them to their logical conclusion? They do not exist, they are no more than mere words, until they are logically developed in this way: there is no half-measure in such matters.'
>
> "This is, of course, all very well: but in life nothing is taken to its ultimate conclusion, life is a half-way house, a place of obligatory compromise; and, in dealing in logical conclusions, a man steps out of life—or so it would be quite legitimate to argue." (95–96)

There is a sense in which René, proudly and perversely, plunges himself into his misery and rushes to meet the void, the "estrangement from the norm of life," which he sees as the revenge for truth. The prose of René's farewells suggests the assured magisterial resignation underlying his sadness—a consolation not afforded Hester—which makes his position more tolerable than his wife's. His last words to Helen are a valediction from "le roi René": fully aware of his grand gesture, he is quite unrepentant and almost welcomes his exile:

> "We must part, Sister, I am afraid we shall not meet again. . . . (I am) going away into a wilderness among so very solid a mass of strangers. And never to come back. Never to come back. . . .
> "The numbers, the mass of strangers, does not matter, they might as well be stones. Indeed, the thicker the mass of stony strangers the deeper the wilderness. Then the fact that Canada is four-fifths an authentic wilderness does not matter. It would be the same emptiness anywhere. The same ghastly void, next door to nothingness." (137)

Those elements of René's histriography which cause most concern are, in a sense, a logical development of his personal beliefs. Lewis solves the difficulty of conveying René's standing as an historian by providing him with a follower—Rotter Parkinson—whose article, "A Historian who is anti-History," is a vindication of René's position (and also, incidentally, of some of Lewis's own views). This interpolated appraisal balances the ignorant vilifications of his detractors and suggests just what it is that René renounces. There is a whole world-view implicit in Harding's ideals: the "New Age" of the Twentieth Century, he believes, has been destroyed by a World War and the widespread acceptance of a divisive Marxist ideology. Not at home in the modern world, René is only too aware of the "incompatibility of the age and his personality."

Defending René against the accusation of *The Times* that he is "fascist minded," Rotter describes him as a "Jansenist," whose dualism sees mankind in terms of "the uncreative majority" and the "inventive and creative few." Not content with merely cataloguing the past, René believes that the historian should make value judgments about it. Contemporary history should not be a Mme. Tussaud's of "important figures," but rather a "chart of the ocean" which illustrates the "big ideologic currents, gaudily coloured, converging, dissolving, combining or contending." Events, because they happened, are not *ipso facto* of importance. The historian's role, like that of the artist, is to look for values in the morass of the past and not merely chronicle the brutalities of the "generations of Caliban."

René's ideas help define his character: the relentless pursuit of the logical conclusion is analogous, in the realm of philosophy, to his "rational" treatment of Hester. Intellectually, husband and wife are totally incompatible: "their marriage had been a bus-accident," but the three year "semi-animal existence" in the Hotel Blundell brings them together in a painfully won intimacy. Their differences are submerged as they exist—as if in a cataleptic trance—in this limbo, an ante-chamber of Hell. Their former life in pre-war London had been economically suggested in the first chapter of the novel: theirs had been a settled world—totally different from the climatic and social frigidity of Momaco. Yet their lethargic London had been lately darkened by "the shadow of 'That Other Man,'" and in the midst of security a note of forboding sounded. The war forecast by René is only months away when they leave for Canada. It will reveal the wildness underlying the stable world—the chaos just below the threshold of civilization. The war makes the inevitability of their predicament in Canada all the more "destined." Hester clings emotionally to the idea of England, but rationally she knows that return is impossible during the war. Their alienation and desolation in Canada is more than homesickness: the Momaco experience becomes a powerful symbol of René's *angst*. In terms of *The Revenge for Love*, René has seen the "false bottom underlying the spectacle of the universe." Not only is Canada desolate, but the old security of London has become desolate; life itself, it seems, is desolate. The elegiac description of their erstwhile home during the Blitz suggests these wider connotations:

> The Blitz, indeed, changed it a great deal: it shook the decaying cement between its bricks, it shook the slates from its roof. Indeed, in the depths of the war-years it became somewhat a wild place. . . . The cellar was full of dead leaves and a wild cat had established its home there, a brood of wild kittens springing about among the

158

leaves. This wild cat so terrorized the tenants that they dared not go down to their trash bins just outside the cellar-door. . . . All in the end had wild cats in their cellars, for civilization never continued long enough to keep the wild cats out—if you call it civilization, René Harding would shout. (14)

Their hotel room is a womb-like retreat from the physical and spiritual cold. The seasons pass at the far side of a plate-glass window; when they do venture out they are blasted by harsh light and the sub-zero temperatures; the cold is "as impossible to keep out as radium . . . it walked through your heart, it dissolved your kidney, it flashed down your marrow and made an icicle of your coccyx." Although their contact with the world outside becomes limited to the friendly inanities of popular radio entertainers, the newspapers, and the gossip of chars, their "astonishingly violent" microcosm is an ever-present reminder of the violence outside. "World Ruin, Act II" grinds on and René is brutally assaulted in the hotel bar; Roosevelt accepts "the rib of a Japanese marine mounted in gold as a paper knife" while in the room below, a French Canadian beats his wife until she screams endlessly:

> [The hotel] was of course crazy—or more accurately it was crazed. It was a highly unstable box, within an equally unstable larger box, which in its turn nestled within a still larger box, of great social instability, profoundly illogical. The degeneration of the . . . Hotel Blundell was but a microcosmic degeneration repeated upon a larger and larger scale, until you reached the enormous instability of the dissolving System, controlling the various States. All this one day, at a touch you would think, no more, would come rushing down in universal collapse.—Indeed, that was what war meant. It was a collapse, a huge cellular destruction of society. It was crazy as this house was crazy. (190)

As physical hardship becomes a way of life, René grows reconciled; he develops "an appetite for this negation of life." He begins to modify his theories and grieves "less over the universal catastrophe as he realized more thoroughly its dark necessity, its innateness." The magnificently cataclysmic fire shatters the dulling security of this world within a world. The terrible beauty of the winter blaze in sub-zero temperatures, where flames and ice unnaturally coexist, and the metamorphosis of their home into a cocoon of fiery ice are an image of the transformation of René and his final transfiguration into a "glacial shell":

> It was a magnificent sight; a block of ice towering over everything in the immediate neighbourhood. It was of course a hollow iceberg. The interior could be inspected through what had been the street-door of the main hotel-building, on Balmoral Street. What René and Hester gazed into was nothing to do with what had been the Hotel Blundell. It was now an enormous cave, full of mighty icicles as much as thirty feet long, and as thick as a tree, suspended from the skeleton of a roof. Below, one looked down into an icy labyrinth: here and there vistas leading the eye on to other caverns: and tunnels ending in mirrors, it seemed. To the right a deep green recess, as if it had been stained with verdigris. (296)

Like England after the war, like René after his traumatic experiences, the fire is at the heart of the novel symbolizing the mutation of all things in time.

Hester sees the fire as an impetus to make the break from Momaco and return to England. René, however, is as obsessively insistent as his wife: neither can give way; their "neuropathic duet" is obviously a fight to the finish. Clutching at straws, he tells Hester that when the war ends they will return to England, and he clings to Furber, his repulsive patron, in a demented attempt to rationalize his *idée fixe*. After the dark night of the intellect, René once again enters into academic life. His discussions with McKenzie force the "rusty dialectical machine" into action; the dispute over René's Nietzschean tendencies balances with Parkinson's article in the first part of the novel: René begins to resemble his former self. Writing articles, giving lectures, he becomes assimilated into Momaco's way of life; Hester sees him as "having gone over to the side of the enemy." Her grief is not lessened by the knowledge that wartime England is less attractive than her nostalgia has painted it: her desire to return is not rational; she cannot be won over by René's arguments, and her answer lies beyond reason.

Those intimations of "absurdity" which so delighted Kerr-Orr are deeply disturbing to René. At the beginning of the novel he compares himself with their affable—though ridiculous—char, Mrs. Harradson:

There was nothing he dreaded so much as the absurd, in himself, a part of his French idiosyncratic legacy, exaggerated if anything in the course of its grafting to a British stock. But his growing sense of the absurd in everything was painful and to suspect its presence in himself supremely uncomfortable. Once or twice he had observed Mrs. Harradson and asked himself if he was a male Mrs. Harradson. What was the rational, after all? Where was one to look for the *norm?* The nervous impetuousness of his movements of which he was perfectly aware, he had once compared with the charlady's. However, he had concluded, with a laugh, if it is a question of the human kind and its essential absurdity, then of course all right, why should I care? In so absurd a place it was hardly likely that he himself could be otherwise than absurd. (29–30)

Lewis had been reading Sartre and Camus for his book *The Writer and the Absolute* (published 1952), and although he expresses many reservations about existentialism—"one of the oddest mass-borrowings in the history of ideas"—his own concept of the absurd has affinities with that of Camus. René's experience in Canada, culminating in the fire and the death of Affie, deepens his recognition of *le néant* underlying all existence. Looking down in the snow at the dead woman, René thought "that he had seen a smile on Affie's face. He could not be sure of this but he thought he had. She had understood the Absurd. So it was that he found himself doing what the firemen thought he was doing; it was a convulsion of meaningless mirth." (289)

This sense of futility suffuses René's thought; his philosophy of history, even, becomes tinged with it:

This problem of problems can be compressed as follows: if one condemns all history as trivial and unedifying, must not all human life be condemned on the same charge? Is not human life too short to have any real values, is it not too hopelessly compromised with the silliness involved in the reproduction of the species, of all the degradations accompanying the association of those of opposite sex to realize offspring? Then the interminable twenty years of growing up (of nurseries, and later years of flogging, of cribbing, of the onset of sex); twenty years of learning to be something which turns out to be nothing. In maturity, the destruction of anything which has value by the enormous mass of what has no value. In other words, the problem of problems is to find anything of value intact and undiluted in the vortex of slush and nonsense: to discover any foothold (however small) in the phenomenal chaos, for the ambitious mind: enough that is uncontaminated to make it worth-while to worry about life at all. And as to condemning the slush and nonsense, the pillage and carnage which we have glorified as "history"; why, that throws us back upon the futility of our daily lives, which also have to be condemned. (351)

Without the consolation of even the most nihilistic philosophy, Hester's attitude announces defeat, "but not resignation." Her suicide—in one sense the proof of René's intimations of the Absurd—is the final articulation of her grief. René reacts to her suicide note in the way he did to Affie's death: "as he began to read, he was softly laughing." Hester's transformation in death lacks the terrible beauty of the ice-fire: like a grotesque, blood-stained *objet trouvé*, she becomes an exhibit in a mortuary. René cannot accept this; his reason collapses and his recuperation in a Catholic seminary represents a "second withdrawal and suspension of the intellectual process, the giving up of being himself." Again René denies the god within him—his mind—and, as an expression of remorse, "buries his reason in the tomb of his wife." From the desolation of the hotel room there had emerged a new René, ready for new responsibilities; but from this second blow there is no recovery: "The Gods cannot strike *twice* and the man survive."

René leaves the seminary "a half-crazed replica of his former self." He can only come to terms with Hester's death by convincing himself of her madness and then driving her out of his mind. But he can never be completely free of the past and, like Mephistopheles out of Hell, his suffering is not localized. " 'There is no peace for me,' " says René to one of the priests, " 'I see a fiery mist wherever I direct my eyes. But the fire is not outside me, the fire is inside my brain.' " To McKenzie, René is a man possessed: "some evil power," he thought, "was responsible for the body of his friend." The diabolical imagery suggests the depths of the traumatic experience: behind the *persona* of the "grief-stricken husband," René experiences the torments of Hell: " 'My brain is burning,' " he tells McKenzie, " 'I have had that sense of a hot devouring something inside my skull.' " Emptied of life, devoid of feeling, René *dies* to his former self, to his past and to

162

Hester. Having experienced Hell, he returns as a dead soul: the ultimate hollow man. The final pages of the novel present René's "death" as essentially tragic: this is the tragedy of the Absurd:

> The fact was that René Harding had stood up to the Gods, when he resigned his professorship in England. The Gods had struck him down. They had humiliated him, made him a laughing-stock, cut him off from all recovery; they had driven him into the wilderness. The hotel fire gave him a chance of a second lease of life. He seized it with a mad alacrity; he was not, he had not been, killed—he had survived the first retaliatory blow—the expulsion, the ostracism. He was still *almost*, and up-to-a-point, his original self, when he and McKenzie were scrutinizing the philosophic foundations of his contemporary literary enterprise; though already he was being shaken by the unceasing psychological pressure of the obsessed Hester. In fact, it had been *then* that the suppression, the battening down, began: he was obliged to push under and hold down the gathering instability and hysteria. When the Gods struck the second time there was, from the moment of the blow, and the days spent in the white silence of the hospital, no chance that he could survive, at all intact. You cannot kill a man twice, the Gods cannot strike *twice* and the man survive. (406)

The novel's conclusion is so brilliantly realized, so inevitable, that it is difficult to see how it could have ended differently; yet Lewis did draft out a plan for Hester and René to return to London after the war. As W. K. Rose has pointed out, this plan would have involved a repetition of the *Rotting Hill* depiction of the post-war "ice-age," and perhaps this was one of the reasons why Lewis abandoned the idea. Certainly the synopsis creates the same *ethos*: "Their reaction to the London of the immediate post-war was of the blackest description. It was like encountering one's oldest friend selling matches in the gutter, with a face altered by disease." René marks exam papers; they again live on the poverty-line; life is the same as in Canada, "with this exception, that there was no Mr. Furber." Hester kills herself in the same manner, but her suicide note explicitly exonerates René: " 'I just cannot bear to see anymore the way you are living, and to think that that is the way you will always have to live. As if you had committed a crime. I know that your crime consists of refusing to accept the world's conditions, to live in a decent way. The way

163

you are living, the way you have been living since you resigned your job, is a punishment for not being a blackguard.' "

In this alternative ending, Rotter Parkinson talks of René as an *übermensch*: " 'At Oxford, a number of us saw in you a leader. You played a great part in our life.' " This superman-*manqué*, in the depths of despair, gives Rotter his reasons for not committing suicide: " 'I have been a historian for so long, I am in the condition of a detective-story-reader; I would like to know how the contemporary "mystery" will turn out.' " This alternative conclusion is, admittedly, only a synopsis, yet it totally lacks the imaginative intensity of the published version with the hopeless, mechanical drift unto death.

Many critics have pointed to *Self Condemned* as a *roman à clef* (see *Wyndham Lewis in Canada, passim*), and one only need glance at the letters of this period to see how closely fiction follows fact. In one sense, the novel is Lewis's *apologia*: like René, his creator felt himself to be an outsider, hounded by the "political Absolute" he had transgressed. In *The Writer and the Absolute*, Lewis states his own position—it could be René writing:

> What has befallen me, or rather my books, proves what is my contention: namely that the mid-20th Century writer is only nominally free, and should not fail to acquire a thorough knowledge of the invisible frontiers surrounding his narrow patch of liberty, to transgress which may be fatal. . . .
>
> Four or five hundred years ago it was the religious Absolute which was the writer's problem. Today it is the political Absolute. (8, 195)

9

The Fiction of Life
After Death

> My little treatise *The Man of the World* has taken longer even to get on its legs than I had expected. I work incessantly at it. I am never in bed before 2, or often later; and for the present dine alone to get it done. (*Letters* 136–137)

Thus, in 1923, Lewis described his work in progress to T. S. Eliot. As first conceived, *The Man of the World* was to be a comprehensive statement in several *genres* of the Lewisian philosophy, but the "little treatise" soon became a *magnum opus*; then, totally unmanageable as a single book, it resulted in those major "Himalayan" works published during the twenties, one of which was *The Childermass* (1928). Twenty seven years elapsed before Lewis added to "Section I" of this work; yet even after the appearance of *Monstre Gai* and *Malign Fiesta*, the book—now entitled *The Human Age*—was still unfinished.

The combination of fantasy and philosophy was first essayed by Lewis in "The Enemy of the Stars" (1914). There, Hanp and Arghol acted out the human drama in a dream-landscape representing life: in *The Childermass* the dream is of death. Observable reality shifts perpetually; solid-state physics are constantly disintegrating; flux is embodied in the new ontology. Everything is in the state of becoming something other; nothing has stability or substance. A tree is just as likely to vanish as are the characters to grow, shrink or change sex. Pulley and Satters, not long dead, find themselves lost in this "parody of eternity" without knowing where they are, or why they are there. "To an agonizing degree," writes I. A. Richards, "we're not allowed to know what it is

165

about." The otherworldly quality of the setting is realized in a hard-edged prose:

> The city lies in a plain, ornamented with mountains. These appear as a fringe of crystals to the heavenly north. One minute bronze cone has a black plume of smoke. Beyond the oasis-plain is the desert. The sand-devils perform up to its northern and southern borders. The alluvial bench has recently gained, in the celestial region, upon the wall of the dunes. The "pulse of Asia" never ceases beating. But the outer Aeolian element has been worsted locally by the element of the oasis.
>
> The approach to the so-called Yang Gate is over a ridge of nummulitic limestone. From its red crest the city and its walls are seen as though in an isometric plan. Two miles across, a tract of mist and dust separates this ridge from the river. It is here that in a shimmering obscurity the emigrant mass is collected within sight of the walls of the magnetic city. To the accompaniment of innumerable lowing horns along the banks of the river, a chorus of mournful messages, the day breaks. At the dully sparkling margin, their feet in the hot waves, stand the watermen, signalling from shore to shore. An exhausted movement disturbs the night-camp stretching on either side of the highway—which when it reaches the abrupt sides of the ridge turns at right angles northward. Mules and oxen are being driven out on to the road: like the tiny scratches of a needle upon this drum, having the horizon as its perimeter, cries are carried to the neighbourhood of the river.
> (*The Childermass*, Calder 1965, 9)

The strange, credible "otherness" of this ambience is achieved by the combination of the totally fantastic with a more familiar iconography of the fabulous. The *milieu* of this physical life-after-death is created from a fusion of emblematic *tableaux* from diverse mythologies set against a background of primary geographical features. These opening paragraphs, like a long, panning camera shot, sketch in the "human" features of city, animals, people—all dwarfed and dominated by the elemental mountains, smoke, desert, dunes, mist and dust. Beelzebub is a reality; Heaven a geographical locale: the unreal is disquietingly familiar. The visually precise imagery ambiguously creates uncertainty and unreality; a whole new world of "things" is created, amidst which Pulley and Satters wander aimlessly. Then, as if the lens were

166

being focused more exactly, perceptions—fantastic, yet under-
standable—emerge from the welter and profusion of details:

> Ahead of them, unnoticed until now, a heavy fly-boat is disembark-
> ing a working-party of the peons dispatched at daybreak from the
> celestial port for field-work and employment in the camp.
>
> Grey-faced, a cracked parchment with beards of a like material,
> ragged wisps and lamellations of the skin, bandage-like turbans of
> the same shade, or long-peaked caps, their eyes are blank, like
> discoloured stones. A number of figures are collected with picks
> and shovels, baulks, a wheelbarrow in the shape of a steep trough,
> a gleaming sickle, two long-handled sledges and one heavy beetle-
> hammer. Their spindle limbs are in worn braided dungaree suitings.
> One holds by the bridle an ass, which trumpets with sedate hysteria.
> Electrified at each brazen blare, its attendant stiffens. He is shaken
> out of an attitude to which on each occasion he returns, throwing
> him into a gaunt runaway perspective, that of a master-acrobat
> tilted statuesquely at an angle of forty-five degrees from the upright
> awaiting the onset of the swarming troupe destined for his head
> and shoulders. SHAM 101 is painted in letters of garnet-red upon
> the hull of the fly-boat. An ape crouches, chained, its hand on the
> tiller. . . .
>
> The ass pumps an ear-splitting complaint into its downy snout,
> scouring the loud sound up and down in an insane seesaw. The
> halter with which he is held seems to have some mechanical
> connection with the performance. Blinking gently and stupidly, he
> then hangs his neck and head over the ground, detached from his
> strange cry. (20–21, 25)

The visual certainty contrasts with the visionary unreality of the
descriptions. The calm tone captures the frightening clarity of an
hallucination; reality is totally distorted, yet, because it cannot
be changed, it must be accepted. Freed from the confines of
verisimilitude, Lewis's characters are bound by no laws; what was
metaphor in, say, descriptions of Bestre's physical enormities, now
becomes "reality." As details pile upon details, this grotesque
wonderland takes shape; much of the action is pure play, and
the creation of the fantasy is the *raison d'être* of its existence.

Pulley and Satters gradually become more aware of their
position in this arid after-life. They are petitioners for salvation
and their present physical form—resulting from a process of
"psychic mummification"—represents their reversion to type.

167

Satters had known Pulley at school, had been, in fact, his "fag"; this new appearance symbolically recreates his essential being:

> Satterthwaite is in knee-cords, football stogies, tasselled golf stockings, a Fair Isle jumper, a frogged mess jacket, a Mons Star pinned upon the left breast, and a Rugby cap, the tinsel rusted, of out-size, canted forward. (12)

Satters, whatever his age, would always be fundamentally child-like—hence his motley accoutrements. Pulley, on the other hand, is more assertive, relatively in command of the situation and, as defined by this existential iconography, is "nanny," "guide" and "master" to his mewling, puking fag. This pair, like a Laurel and Hardy version of Don Quixote and Sancho Panza, stagger across the plain of Niflheim, "home of the mist," in prescient parody of a lunar walk.

This version of "reality" is a many-faceted comic critique of the Bergsonian concept of *la durée*, Alexander's notion of "Time as the soul of space," and Whitehead's idea of "eternal objects" which "haunt time like a spirit"—all attacked as fallacies in *Time and Western Man* (1927). In the latter, Lewis exposes the "anti-physical" tendencies of the time-philosophers, and his characterization of the Bergsonian world describes very well the instability of Niflheim: "Chairs and tables, mountains and stars, are animated into a magnetic restlessness and sensitiveness, and exist on the same vital terms as man. They are as it were the lowest grade, the most sluggish of animals. All is alive: and, in that sense, all is mental" (449). In this world of the continuous present, Time has usurped Space; psychology has triumphed over objective reality: "Nothing is, but thinking makes it so."

As if to illustrate how ridiculous is *la durée*, Lewis creates another equally fantastic Time-Space relationship. After staggering through the hazardous, glutinous embodiment of Bergsonism, Satters and Pulley come upon a "time-hallucination." They walk back into the Eighteenth Century and Pully feels that he is " 'built for Time-travel. . . . I'm in my element.' " Satters, however, has a tantrum and, like a vicious child ignorant of his own strength, tramples to death a defenceless Tom Paine. It is with a nice ironical twist that Satters, after his jackboot dismissal

of the author of *The Rights of Man*, is next faced with an autocratic and seemingly omnipotent Bailiff. " 'There is no rule of
law,' " he tells the crowd, " 'you are absolutely without rights
independently of my will.' "

At first, the Bailiff is as much an enigma as everything else in
The Childermass. Pulley tells Satters, " 'He's the best hated man
anywhere,' " but his origin and role are a complete mystery:

> "Some say he is Jacobus del Rio, some a Prince of Exile, I have
> heard him called Trimalchio Loki Herod Karaguez Satan, even some
> madman said Jesus, there is no knowing what he is. I believe he's
> just what you see, himself, he is the Bailiff simply, I don't under-
> stand the insistence on something factitive behind him or why he is
> not accepted as he is." (72)

It soon becomes clear, however, that the Bailiff is the "great
administrative officer," deciding who shall be "saved" and enter
the Magnetic City. He holds court in the Camp just outside the
gates of the city, hearing the petitions of those who would enter
this "antechamber of salvation." A burlesque of Peter at the gates
of Heaven, the Bailiff performs in a booth resembling a Punch and
Judy theatre: " 'It is God's will that the utmost fairness should
mark the proceedings . . . anybody who is so disposed can hold
us up.' " The final half of the novel describes these hold-ups: the
Bailiff listens and talks interminably as various characters raise
abstruse philosophical points requiring abstruse philosophical
answers.

As one of the "Princes of Time," the Bailiff declares himself
" 'primitive and proud of it.' " Pot-bellied and hunchbacked, he
is a grotesque personification of the *Zeitgeist*—both in the sense
of Spirit of the Times and also The Spirit of Time—and a composite
of much that Lewis detested. " 'Le mob c'est moi,' " he declares,
and his *obiter dicta* bristle with catchwords of figures hated by
Lewis. Set-questions from the appellants allow Lewisian predilections to be explored: " 'What is the difference,' " the Bailiff is
asked, " 'between Space-Time and Space and Time?' " Sometimes
serious, more often wildly comic, the badinage weaves amongst
the implications and niceties of such questions, with the Bailiff,
of course, always showing his true colours as Time-philosopher
par excellence:

"Eternity is in love with the productions of Time," announces the Bailiff. "Some of you disregard your debt to Time in a really unaccountable way. Time is the mind of Space—Space is the mere body of Time. Time is life, Time is money, Time is all good things!— Time is God!" (229)

Pulley and Satters, like a composite Everyman, are very much onlookers at this dialectical jousting. As a curtain-raiser to the great debates with the Hyperideans, the Bailiff disputes with Tormod Macrob, a lugubrious Scot, who avails himself of the appellant's right to catechize the gate-keeper. To a mocking background chorus of " 'Kiltie! Look Kiltie, they're coming doon mon—aye it's not decent,' " Macrob persists in questioning his ontological status:

"Am I an entity? Can I be put into Space and Time or taken out again, as you would put a pea into a glass of water and take it out again? Do I belong to empirical existence: or am I something apart from that, joined to it for a moment?" (224)

The Bailiff cavalierly handles the questions of this "Stammer of Space-Time" and, like a good time-cultist, by reducing Macrob's existence to a series of physical contingencies and sense-states, he totally obliterates the Scotsman's self.

Enraged by his sophistical dismissal, Macrob retaliates with pantomimic directness and the debate disintegrates into farcical Punch and Judy violence:

The slow mind of Macrob leaves its shell inch by inch, horned blind and dazzled: then it is out, the shell stands apart statuesquely from its soul at last, staring and stark for a queasy second, and the unmitigated Macrob-clansman clicks into action. The muscular shell springs back, rebounds from the barrier (as it would look to the child-eye checking the event) and, intelligent gutta-percha missile, darts headlong in reverse and catapults up, a bolt from the abyss, in an animal parabola-on-its-back straight at its appointed target, its bull's-eye the Bailiff. With a rattle and shock the charging body crashes into the bema which it tosses back half-a-foot upon its socket in the volcanic rock, the fletched topknot oscillating like an instrument set to register such upheavals: up sweeps the gaunt Scottish arm with beaked talon and then thumb and index snap-to-upon the snish-tickled twitching snout, wallowing in its black bath of snuff. The powder from the snuff-box, batted upwards, explodes

170

into the Bailiff's face, blackened like that of a man doctored by an apache on the sneeze-racket, and the body of the squealing nose is stuck fast like a fat rat in a trap.

As a dog with a rat seeking to stun it the Macrob tugs the nose violently this way and that.

"Aiiiiiiiii mmmurder! Mummummu*mur*-ddd-er!" (235)

Like Tom Paine, Macrob is trampled into the ground by Bailiffites. After the orgiastic convulsions of snuff and expressionist brutality, Hyperides—always remaining above the *mêlée*—takes up the burden of opposition to his "legendary enemy," the Bailiff. They are the "oldest opposites in the universe," and the "Classical" Hyperides sees the Bailiff's apotheosis of Time as a surrender to the "sensational chaos":

"Is not your Space-Time for all practical purposes only the formula recently popularized to accommodate the empirical sensational chaos? Did not the human genius redeem us for a moment from that, building a world of human-divinity above that flux? Are not your kind betraying us again in the name of exact research to the savage and mechanical nature we had overcome; at the bidding, perhaps, of your maniacal and jealous God?"

". . . Also some God release us soon from your demented itch for what you call *action*, from the insane fuss and rattle of your common, feverish, unhappy mind! That Time-factor that our kinsman the Greek removed and that you have put back to obsess, with its movement, everything—to put a jerk and a wriggle, a tic and a grimace, everywhere—what is that accomplishing except the breaking-down of all our concrete world into a dynamical flux, whose inhuman behests we must follow, instead of it waiting on us? *An eternity of intoxication!*—the platonic description of it— that is your great promise." (155, 156)

Hyperides here voices the basic thesis that Lewis affirms throughout his polemical writings on this subject, and Hyperides's attack on the Bailiff is identical with Lewis's attack on Bergson: as time-philosophers, both are "recommending capitulation to the material *in struggle against* which the greatest things in the world have been constructed" (*The Art of Being Ruled*, 391).

"Floridly, fiercely and irresponsibly," the Bailiff pronounces his anti-intellectualism: " 'I prefer,' " he brags with Lawrentian directness, " 'hot-blood to your beastly intellects.' " Again,

171

Hyperides states the Classical position as opposed to the visceral philosophy of gut-reactions. Hyperides is for the eye, the intellect and concrete reality; he tells the Bailiff:

> "When you begin thinking you lie down and close your eyes that is true. In your discourse you philosophers always speak as though men were heavily-muffled thickly-myopic percipient automata: you show them peering into a metaphysical fog in which they intuit painfully and dimly in the black recesses of their neural regions the forms and utterances of other men. What could be further from the truth? The whole universe except at night is brilliantly electro-magnetically illuminated. Men can examine each other and note every muscular change, every flash of an eyelash, with the utmost distinctness. There is between the percipient and the object, when that object is a human organism, the closest contact of the spirit, because of this brilliant physical light." (317)

This "brilliant physical light"—also an important feature of Lewis's early style—pierces the metaphysical fog of these misbegotten philosophies, illuminating the conceptual and corporeal world of the Bailiff for what it is.

Time dominates *The Childermass*: the wanderings of Pulley and Satters *in* it, and their listening *to* it, are base lines from which Lewis conducts occasional "enemy" sorties into other aspects of contemporary culture. In the early stages of the novel, Pulley and Satters are satiric weapons in a series of critical attacks upon James Joyce and Gertrude Stein. There are several biographical parallels between Joyce and Pulley; and Satters, like Dan and Lady Fredigonde in *The Apes of God*, stutters and "steins" continually. Lewis had already, in *Time and Western Man*, submitted Gertrude Stein's style to a devastating analysis, and quoted her on her own *Melanctha*:

> I created then a prolonged present naturally I know nothing of a continuous present but it came naturally to me to make one, it was simple it was clear to me and nobody knew why it was done like that, I did not myself although naturally to me it was natural.

The banal, repetitive recitative of the infantile Satters burlesques this technique:

> Pulley has been most terribly helpful and kind there's no use excusing himself Pulley has been most terribly helpful and kind—

most terribly helpful and he's been kind. He's been most terribly kind and helpful, there are two things, he's been most kind he's been terribly helpful, he's kind he can't help being—he's terribly. He's been most fearfully tiresome when he likes and he's been tiresome too but who doesn't when they're not? He has been most terribly. (44)

In a typically Lewisian *reductio ad absurdum*, this mannerism is extended to include not only phrases and words, but even syllables:

"Oblige me by not behaving like a blag-blaggar-ger-guard! Yes you y-y-you, th-though you pretend to be far-away! Y-y-you damned old Cis-ciss-cissy! Yes you Mister—Pullman!"

Pullman coughs: a scandalized rigor descends upon the averted face.

"Y-y-y-y-y-y-you howwid blag-blag-blag-blag-blag-blag-blag-blag-blag-blag——!"

A stein-stammer that can never reach the *guard* of blackguard hammers without stopping *blag*.

Pullman puts his fingers in his ears, shutting out the blagging which passes over into high-pitched continuous stammering, and the fingers are removed with a quiet precision. Satters begins screaming hoarsely, violently hurling his head towards Pullman to drive home *blag bug* or *bag* with panting whistling discharges. (63–64)

This deliberate cultivation of naïvety and verbal anarchy—sabotaging the sentence, spiking the verb, as it is called in *One-Way Song*—is what Lewis terms the "dark stammering voice of social dissolution." The Bailiff, too, is an enemy of the *logos*: " 'If there is one thing we hate more than an *image*,' " he tells Potter the artist, " 'it is a *word*.' "

As an incarnation of the *Zeitgeist*, the Bailiff can transform himself into any of its facets, and most of these metamorphoses illustrate his "primitive and proud of it" boast. His baby-talk to the Bailiffites dramatizes the endless inanities of the "youth" *motif* anathematized by Lewis in *Doom of Youth* (1932). Just as the stein stutter is pursued to its ultimate conclusion, so is the cult of youth (of "Messrs. Winn and Waugh" and the age suffragettes), taken to absurd extremes. He tells his noisy followers:

173

"Do keep quiet you naughty boys, I s'all have to spank oo if oo won't mind me else so-there!—pam-pam on Tomtit's big bad bold and bonny bot-bot of a B.T.M.! For two pins I'd short-coat you scut of smutty crazy shavers and send you in with bottle and crib in layettes and binders." (170)

The baby-talk modulates into the patois of *Nigger Heaven*: "'What's zat,'" says the Bailiff "'but ze ganz same ding als baby-wallow.'" Continually retreating from the rational, the Bailiff uses language as ambiguously and idiosyncratically as possible; he represents the "organized hatred of the intellect" as defined in *The Art of Being Ruled*. "Liberty is manufactured with words," wrote Lewis in that book. "All our struggles are about words; for no one would fight for reality, since without a name they would not be able to recognize it" (372). The jazz rhythms of the negro prose slip and slide around meaning; words, here, are furthest from being symbols of the intellect, becoming, rather, the effluent of emotional and physiological processes. The Bailiff's torchlight exploration of his glottal machinery, his pride in the subconscious where "dark words are dancing," reveal him to be a man of "the dark within":

> [The Bailiff] stretches open his gills, seizes his fungus-tongue to liven it up and make it hop, and directs the light of an electric torch inside.
> BAILIFF: "Seen my prattling-chete—it's pretty! Seen my talking-tools honey?"
> He prods the torch-button, the light snaps out and snaps back several times.
> BAILIFF: "Seen this Kit, tongue lips glottis and velum all one penny-rattle! an that ole parrot-tongue he clappers on as he's taught—habit—habit he's a good clapper."
> He strokes its dark fur with a finger-tip.
> BAILIFF: "How worms talk in sounding-boxes—it's too marvellous Kit! Come now and I'll show you how it is that the words get melted, in glandmud-washing of de Swanee-bottom. I'll explain the last, that's the mud-flats where the dark words are dancing—I can't show them you—they get swamped." (172–173)

This "preoccupation with the *vitals* of things" is yet another fictionalization of a major theme in *The Art of Being Ruled*, where "the smoking hot *inside* of things" is contrasted with the "hard, cold, formal skull or carapace":

> The *emotional* of the bergson dogma is the heat, moisture, shapelessness, and tremor of the vitals of life. The *intellectual* is the ectodermic case, the ideality of the animal machine *with its skin on.*
>
> Finally, the bergsonian (jamesesque psycho-analytic, wagnerian Venusberg) philosophy of the hot *vitals*—of the blood-stream, of vast cosmic emotion, gush and flow—is that of a *blind* organism. There are no eyes in that philosophy. It *sees* no more than the embryo: it is hardly yet male or female: it is sightless and neuter. It is the creed of a sightless, ganglionic mass, in short: and as such invites to that "eternity of intoxication" of the gibe of Plato. (403)

The Bailiff's speech finally deteriorates into an almost solipsistic, incommunicable idiom—the language, in fact, of Joyce's *Finnegans Wake*. Occasioned by purely physiological stimuli—a rap on the funnybone effects his "brain pan," which "bin and mixt all the lettas"—the result is a stream of "wormeaten wordies infant-bitten and granfer-mumbled." With multi-level Joycean puns, the Bailiff's outpouring both exemplifies and criticizes the "brain-weed and word-fungle" of "Master Joys of Potluck, Joys of Jingles, whom men call Crossword-Joys for his apt circum-solutions but whom the gods call just Joys or Shimmy, shut and short." Alluding to what he sees as Joyce's self-publicity at Sylvia Beach's *Shakespeare and Company* bookshop, Lewis portrays this "gilt-edged conshie of a playboy of westend letters" as the darling of the fashionable *avant-garde*:

> "*Sweet Will* as shop-sign is the best high-brow stop-sign—to say *We have* that Swan of Avon *right here inside* with us for-keeps, beard brogue pomes and all (in a hundred inedited poses from youth up to be seen on all hands tastefully snapshotted) ponderating 'Neggs-in-progress' and 'wirk-on-the-way' in our back office (with Vico the mechanical for guide in the musty labrinths of the latter-days to train him to circle true and make true orbit upon himself) so STOP!—but there is more in confidence, for twixt me you the shop sign and crooked counter Sweet Will is all very well but for tourists only, and there are others, non-tripping, that are surely stopping and wanting and quite otherwise wanting. So our sign's

reversible—get me? there is a fourth dimension of introverted Swans of Avon unseen by the profane, we have *that* in the shop *too* ant many narfter thorts as well as swan-songs, so walk right in we'd be glad to be met by you." (175–176)

Although, to the reader, the Bailiff's harlequinade represents a grotesque perversion of life and a fantastic speeding up of that "ant-like process" which Lewis saw as undermining all cultural activities, Pulley is attracted to his flamboyant vitality. " 'I like the begga,' " he tells Satters with a touch of self-congratulation at his generosity. The novel ends abruptly *in medias res* with the Bailiff's *cortège* returning to the city, while Pulley and Satters, stepping out briskly, "go nowhere." It was to be twenty-seven years before Lewis added to *The Human Age*.

In *Monstre Gai*, the travellers enter Third City and Pullman's question, " 'Is this Heaven?' " is soon answered. A less volatile limbo than outside the walls, Third City is a "degenerate, chaotic, outpost of Heaven." The friendly Mr. Mannock gives them the lie of the land: Third City is a super-efficient Welfare State, architecturally well-planned and apparently smoothly-run by "competent bureaucrats." There is an after-death pension, allowing the recipient to benefit from all the amenities of this up-to-date cosmopolitan society. There are, however, limits to the good life offered by Third City: " 'There is no meat, no women, no alcohol, no telephones (except public ones in the street), practically no taxi-cabs, and so on.' " To which a cheerful Pullman replies that " 'it sounds like life on the Falkland Islands.' "

Called "The Heaven of the Young," the city is like a nightmare from *Doom of Youth*: vast herds of ex-humanity, drugged by the smoothness of their "life," exist in "suspended animation, sexless, vegetarian, and dry." Just as Pullman was never sure of what was happening outside the gates, so, at first, is he similarly troubled inside Third City. " 'What is not clear,' " he says to Mannock, " 'is why this place is here, and what the devil we are doing in it.' " The expressionist fantasy of *The Childermass* disappears in the two sequels: a fantasy world is created, but the element of "play" involves external reality rather than the externalized projections of characters' attitudes and ideas. Lewis's prose, too, becomes less the visually precise lexical canvas of his earlier style, and more a strictly referential medium. The

176

brush-strokes of this later style (as seen also in *Rotting Hill*) are less highly-worked and, in a sense, less important than the "subject" they portray. The detective-story interest of what happens next is much more pronounced; the fictionalization of alien philosophies ceases, and the interest centres upon Pullman's actions and reactions in the moral drama.

As the uncertainties of "perhaps, perhaps not," become less frequent, a pattern does gradually emerge and the nature of this "half-way house to Heaven" becomes clearer. Once functional as a testing-place for Salvation, Third City has now lost its rationale and has an uncertain existence midway between Heaven and Hell. The Bailiff was originally the gate-keeper but, having been enormously powerful, he has usurped much of the authority of the putative ruler, the Padishah. The Devil, who has "challenged the Great Architect of the Universe before," has designs upon the city, and soon after Pullman and Satters arrive it is bombarded by hellish artillery. It is from another such Blitz that they will finally flee with the Bailiff—the "gay monster" of the title.

Appearing at first in a continuation of the eclectic harlequinade of *The Childermass*, he bears the symbols of "The Great Fish, a manner of referring to Jesus Christ" and also "the number 666" —the beast of *Revelations*! Without changing his nature, the Bailiff drops the fancy dress and becomes suave and sophisticated —much less of a pantomime character: "he was now a very different person from the barbaric, theatrical figure of the Camp. He was dressed in a dinner-jacket, with a soft white shirt, and wide scarlet ribbon of some order appearing above his waistcoat and crossing his stomach, while in his hand he held a large Havana cigar." The Padishah's liberal, *laissez-faire* tolerance has allowed the Bailiff to set up a vast network of criminal activities from bootlegging to brothel-keeping. The continuous power-struggle between the Bailiff and the "beautiful, ineffectual angel" is a reflection of the eternal conflict between "the great Mazdean Principles of Light and Dark, of the Good and the Bad":

> "Before the modern age, yes, back in the Age of Faith, there was a Heaven and there was a Hell. There was a Heaven of dazzling white, and there was a good coal-black Hell. . . . Well, let us get back to the great changes which have taken place. As we all know, and can see for ourselves, the *Good* and the *Bad* are blurred, are

they not, in the modern age? We no longer see things in stark black and white. We know that all men are much the same. An amoralist . . . such is the modern man. And in the same way in these supernatural regions. It is a terrible come-down all round. What was once the Devil (to whom one 'sold one's soul' and so forth) well today, he is a very unconvinced *devil*, and our Padishah, as we call him, he is a very unconvinced Angel. I know *both*, so I know what I am talking about." (112–113)

Without the security afforded by absolutes, Pullman looks to cruder criteria in choosing his allegiances and, as on earth, he throws in his lot with the "worldly" Bailiff. Just as the physical form of the postulants represents a reversion to type, so too is this moral choice symbolic.

> He had lived with the Bailiff upon the earth but had not recognised him. He had built all his success upon Bailiff-like rather than Padishah-like interests; and now, here, the Bailiff had acted as a magnet: he had been drawn in that direction at once. (223)

It is Pullman's trust in the intelligence which persuades him to follow the Bailiff. The Padishah—on the side of the angels, but "devoid of the slightest trace of gumption"—is not at all attractive. The Bailiff's dialectical dexterity has, inside Third City, been channelled into brutal gangster activities: the charming exterior masks a diabolical viciousness. The allegorical implications of Pullman's dilemma are obvious. Cushioned by the hedonistic luxury of the Phanuel Hotel, and compulsively following his own interests, Pullman drifts into evil. He is quite aware of the Bailiff's nature, yet, moving from "adherent" to "agent," he becomes increasingly involved in the Bailiff's affairs.

Writing about *The Childermass* in *Rude Assignment*, Lewis remarked that its politics had "no relation to those of the earth" —the same could not be said of *Monstre Gai*. Third City's Welfare State is an extrapolation of the "reality" he portrayed in *Rotting Hill*, and the political extremists, haranguing the crowds with familiar rhetoric, are also caricatures of earthly originals. Vogel, "whose only diet was Marx and cabbage," is the Third City Communist; Father Ryan stands for tradition and theocracy; Hyperides—the "Classicist" of *The Childermass*—is now overtly fascist, "hated and disliked by everybody." The Bailiff, who is hardly a political figure in the conventional sense of that word, is more powerful than any of these: he represents "gangster-wealth at its most irresponsible."

A particularly anarchic period of Bailiffite mob-rule culminates in the violent death of Hyperides. His symbolic murder is a horrible parody of the crucifixion, and the scene images the brutality inherent in all power-politics. The changing concept of Hyperides also mirrors a change in Lewis's own political attitude. The authoritarian "Classicism" of the Hyperides in *The Childermass* turns, in *Monstre Gai*, to fascism, and is totally rejected by the moral vision of the fiction:

> The Gay Monster, in his dark-curtained puppet-stage, danced like a lunatic, shooting out his arms and tearing off his beard. The followers of Hyperides with a roar rushed towards the black pall of smoke within which their Master was now invisible. Then suddenly the black smoke parted, exactly like two long black curtains being pulled aside. Within, and now visible to all, was the figure of Hyperides, his beard sheared off below the chin, an enormous nail driven through his throat, behind entering the thick board against which he had stood; on his head was stuck a white pointed hat tied beneath his chin. FOOL was painted on it. (237)

Pressed from within the city by the Padishah, and from without by the Devil's hosts who are attempting to win Third City, the Bailiff is forced to flee to the more amenable Matapolis. Pullman is so far involved with his boss that he and Satters accept the offer of succour. Worried by the description of these realms, Pullman quizzes the Bailiff:

> "Your Excellency, is that old-world city you are describing by any chance Hell?"
> "There is no such place as Hell," was the Bailiff's answer. "It is, believe me, a myth. It is very curious how this 'Hell' story came into being. But do let me assure you, Pullman, there is no such place. Hell is a stupid superstition."
> Pullman looked very coldly at his patron. "Very well," he said. "We will think of your birthplace as a jolly little seaside town, very quaint and picturesque."
> "No, Pullman, it is not like Torquay—I do not say that . . . it is like a very miniature bit of Birmingham painted over to resemble Le Havre." (245–246)

179

It is, of course, Hell; and the pipe-smoking, "liberalized" Sammael, who enjoys Hollywood films, is a very up-to-date Devil.

With the ease of Alice stepping through the looking-glass, the three travellers are transported at the speed of light to Matapolis. Acting in a similar expository role to Mr. Mannock, Madame Heracopoulos, the Bailiff's mother, sets the scene of *Malign Fiesta*. Sinners from earth are transported to the punishment cells at Dis where specialists devise suitable perpetual torments for them. The class-structure of this "metropolis of inquisition" is precisely defined, Lewis's cosmogenic genealogies reading like footnotes to the *Apocrypha*. Angeltown accommodates thirty thousand of the two hundred thousand angels of Matapolis, some of whom were among the original insurgents who left Heaven with Satan. The Devil himself, "Sammael is the name we use for him here," is a terrifying combination of charm and evil, austerity and viciousness.

> The most fundamental thing about Sammael was his puritanism, taking with it, in his case, an intellectual seriousness. But this astute politician no doubt knew that the Puritan was not a popular fellow. Consequently he affected a gayer, a more ostentatious allure than was natural to him. It was as if Cromwell had introduced some lace into his costume, and purchased a gold-headed cane. (126)

Just as the politics of Third City are a reflection of those on earth, so is Hell an extension of all that is hellish in life. The friendly and witty Sammael (who hopes Pullman does not "object to shaking hands with the Devil"), with great pride shows the latter around a Hell which is a combination of Dante's *Inferno* and Auschwitz. " 'I maintain an excellent Hell,' " says Sammael, and his engaging urbanity makes a disturbing contrast with his inhumanity towards a "female sinner" he feeds to lecherous, ravenous carnivores:

> There was her body, shoulder-high, for the fraction of a second, in the midst of the stinking pack—the sickening odour increasing in intensity. Just for that fractional speck of time a dozen claws could be seen defiling her person. The most terrible scream Pullman had ever heard filled aurally that speck of time. . . .
>
> "As you may have realized, the beasts soon kill the women, they are so violent. As they fornicate, they eat. They bite mouthfuls out of them, regardless of the fact that, with the human, death is found a very short distance beneath the surface." (57, 59)

Accompanied by Dr. Hachilah, Pullman tours the "Surgery of Morals" where wounds are kept fresh and "just" torments are devised. Underlying the up-dating of Dante and the macabre *Pit and Pendulum* ingenuity, is a very real sense of the physically revolting nature of evil. By means of implicit parallels with Nazi atrocities, Lewis creates a concentration-camp world which stands as a terrifying objective correlative of Sammael's self confessed " 'abhorrence of Man and his abominable playmate Woman.' " It is this horror which Pullman—the not unsympathetic Everyman character—endorses.

While the inane Satters tickles friendly angels and plays with his Sizzle Wizzle, he increasingly becomes a mere appendage to his mentor. Pullman himself is more and more involved with Sammael, his rise in status is gauged by his new relationship with the Bailiff. The latter, now diminutively called "Zoë," is magnanimously helped by Pullman, the Director of Angeltown's University and Sammael's most trusted counsellor. In the projected creation of "The Human Age" Pullman's machiavellian abilities are given full scope; he even out-devils Sammael.

The master-plan to "humanize" the angels is an attempt to terminate the servility of Hell to Heaven by ending the supernatural role of the diabolic powers. Sammael conjectures that by abolishing one half of the Manichean dualism, he would ultimately bring about "the annihilation of the Divine." Pullman is ever at his master's side to allay his fears, encourage, and give advice. On the change of status from angelic to human, Pullman suggests a gradual introduction of the ways of man to the divine. A great party is arranged—the "malign fiesta" of the title—and to encourage the angels to consort with women, at Pullman's instigation, the profoundly misogynist Sammael is accompanied by a supposed "fiancée" (of whom he brutally disposes when she proves unsuitable). Pullman believes that the outcome of all this could be " 'a superb Human Age . . . where all the high activities could blossom,' " but in reality the fiesta is the epitome of holiday-camp vulgarity: bands, confetti, masks, postiche noses, false moustaches, fancy hats, wine, women, song, and still more women.

Fleetingly, in *Malign Fiesta*, there are intimations of another reality which contrasts absolutely with the ways of Sammael. Pullman has glimpses of this, but is so far implicated in the Devil's

181

work, that he can do no more than occasionally and furtively pray. This paradoxical recourse to prayer, even while engaged in the pursuit of evil, is not a self-preservatory ploy: it represents a response to his predicament which runs deeper than the pragmatic search for "worldly" advancement. Far from denying the existence of God, Pullman is profoundly in awe of His might: *Malign Fiesta* presents this spiritual paradox. In this "nightmarish existence where the supernatural is the real," Pullman's doubts, fears and allegiances—as if in a modern Morality play—are embodied in his relationships with the Bailiff, Sammael and, finally, with God. Just when The Human Age seems feasible, God intervenes, sending a message which threatens Pullman, in spite of his conciliatory prayers, with "eternal damnation." An all-out attack is launched upon Hell; right prevails, and this section ends with Pullman being "carried away by two of God's soldiers."

The conclusion of the tetralogy was to have dealt with Pullman in Heaven, but, as Lewis wrote to D. G. Bridson, "God is a big problem": it was a problem he never solved. In *The Human Age*, God had so far remained behind the scenes—like an ultimate Pierpoint figure—but Heaven without Him would be like *Hamlet* without the Prince. In the opening scenes of an early (and seemingly rejected) draft of *The Trial of Man*, God is described by the Hospital Director as " 'a very charming gentleman.' " He goes on, " 'I offered him a cigarette, he smiled and shook his head.' " Sammael as a sophisticated, dinner-jacketed, pipe-smoking man's man had been a complete success: God Almighty as a similarly up-dated man about town—albeit a non-smoker—was fraught with problems. For whatever reasons, rather than work on *The Trial of Man*, Lewis chose to complete *The Red Priest* and begin another novel (*Twentieth Century Palette*)—the book on which he was still working when he died.

Conclusion

In these readings of Lewis's fictions, I have stressed their polemical designs and suggested some of their recurrent themes. This concentration upon fiction as philosophy is deliberate: it seems to me to be the way in which most of Lewis's fiction demands to be read. His attitude to the "sacred office" of the novelist was, to say the least, unconventional, and to evaluate his fiction by means of a preconceived poetics of the novel does Lewis no justice. In his attempt to reconcile fiction and philosophy, he was as radical an innovator in literature as he was in painting. Although antithetical to D. H. Lawrence in almost every conceivable way, Lewis's rethinking of the ends and means of fiction was as fundamental as Lawrence's. Where the latter wished to channel the reader's "passional sympathetic consciousness," Lewis worked for a cerebral response: the novels and stories which resulted from these aesthetics—although diametrically opposed in all else—are alike in their rejection of accepted form. Lewis's imaginative writing can be as dialectical as Brechtian "Epic Theatre," and it is as irrelevant to invoke Flaubert in criticizing Lewis's lack of form as it is to cite "the well-made play" against Brecht.

Lewis's didactic intent is apparent throughout his imaginative writing: from the "super-real" dialectic of "The Enemy of the Stars," through the ironic pedagogy of Tarr and the flawed *übermenschen*, the gargantuan satires of the twenties, the social and political satires of the thirties, the late "non-fiction fiction," to the new mythology of *The Human Age*, Lewis waged his one-man campaign against the intellectual lassitude of the age. Often reading like modern Socratic dialogues, Lewis's fictions are peopled with characters who represent attitudes or philosophies. Action

183

becomes a function of a particular world-view and in this way ideas are evaluated according to the behaviour of their embodiment. "The orthodox Flaubertian groans," wrote Ezra Pound, "when Mr. Lewis springs . . . several pages of dogma or argument quite likely to be Mr. Lewis's own"; Pound then goes on to show how wrong the orthodox Flaubertian can be: Lewis, he claims, belongs to that species of "English outsizers" who, rather than following precepts, create their own.

Lewis's work can be read as a defence of Western Man against the forces of the anti-Enlightenment which, he felt, so many of his contemporaries espoused. Were Lewis alive today he would find the post-Beckettian withdrawal into a near solipsistic silence as inimical as were the consciously "irrational" extravagances of Dada or the atavistic primitivism of Lawrence. Much of what Lewis detested and opposed has, in fact, come to full flower in the post-Modernist era: "random authors" like Brion Gysin and William Burroughs, who believe that "to speak is to lie" and who exalt the psychedelic *objet trouvé* into an art-form, represent a realization of the Bailiff's worst literary excesses. Jean Genet's submissive cry (in *Our Lady of the Flowers*) epitomizes one aspect of this philosophy of abandonment: "The only way to avoid the horror of horror is to give in to it." One might take all of Lewis's work as an attempt to face up to existence—horror and all—and to create meaning, discover values, in the phenomenal chaos: one must *never* give in to it.

As a satirist, Lewis is in the tradition of Pope and Swift; he is, indeed, the only satirist of modern times who can stand the comparison with these Augustans. Like them, Lewis attacked individuals as well as vices, and his most memorable satiric fictions are those—like *The Childermass*, *The Apes of God* and *The Revenge for Love*—in which he sets up satiric victims and then, with imaginative viciousness, proceeds to destroy them. Alongside this demolition work runs a strong sense of the satirist's duty to society. Lewis would have agreed with Shaw that "the salvation of the world depends on the men who will not take evil good-humouredly, and whose laughter destroys the fool instead of encouraging him." Lewis's "Enemy" attitude carried over into life the traditional *persona* of the satirist; an account of his feud with Bloomsbury is included in this study as the epitome of this role.

The "public bodyguard" obviously relished his task and was not above looking at himself with irony:

> As once upon a time, according to English law, it was the duty of any man, observing another rustling a horse, to apprehend him (if he could) and to hang him (if he had a rope) to the nearest tree (if there was one thereabouts): so it was encumbent on all good citizens to turn satirists on the spot . . . if they had any satire in them, of which I happened to have an adequate supply.

In addition to the castigation of the especially wicked or the peculiarly foolish, satire was for Lewis a way of looking at humanity. Man, that animal with the word-habit, was an endless source of fascination, and man's self-pride was an endless source of satirical material. From *The Wild Body* to *Rotting Hill*, Lewis sardonically presents both individual psychologies and group dynamics for our instruction, delight and scorn.

The term "fiction of ideas" has, perhaps, too many associations with the "conversation novels" of Norman Douglas or Aldous Huxley to be of much value when describing Lewis's best fiction. His imaginative polemics share the same concern for the "life of the intelligence" that is manifested in the proselytising, discursive writing, and this all-embracing Lewisian *credo* is explicitly voiced in the preface to *Time and Western Man*:

> I have said to myself that I will fix my attention upon these things that have most meaning for me. All that seems to me to contradict or threaten those things I will do my best to modify or defeat, and whatever I see that favours and agrees with those things I will support and do my best to strengthen.

This seriousness of intent is everywhere apparent in Lewis's fiction. His vision of life can be profoundly disturbing, and it often seems that the function of his art is less to create illusions than to destroy them. Ezra Pound, one of Lewis's most perceptive critics, pointed to that side of Lewis's genius which is very relevant today:

> It is of inestimable value that there be men who receive things in a modality different from one's own; who correlate things one would not oneself have correlated. The richness of any given period depends largely upon the number and strength of such men.

185

Selected Bibliography

Primary Sources

"The Pole," *The English Review*, 2 (May, 1909), 255–65.

"Some Innkeepers and Bestre," *The English Review*, 2 (June, 1909), 471–84.

"Unlucky for Pringle," *The Tramp: an Open Air Magazine*, (February 1911), pp. 404–14.

"A Man of the Week: Marinetti," *The New Weekly*, 1, No. 11 (May 30, 1914), 328–9.

Blast No. 1. (June 20, 1914), London, John Lane, the Bodley Head.

Blast No. 2, War Number (July 1915), London, John Lane, the Bodley Head.

"The French Poodle," *The Egoist*, 3 No. 3 (March 1, 1916), 39–41.

The Ideal Giant, The Code of a Herdsman, Cantleman's Spring-Mate, privately printed for the *Little Review*, 1917.

Tarr. London, The Egoist Ltd., 1918.

"The War Baby," *Art and Letters*, 2, No. 1 (Winter 1918), 14–41.

"Sigismund," *Art and Letters*, 3, No. 1 (Winter 1920), 14–31.

The Tyro: A Review of the Arts of Painting, Sculpture, and Design, No. 1, London, The Egoist Press, 1921.

The Tyro: A Review of the Arts of Painting, Sculpture, and Design, No. 2, London, The Egoist Press, 1922.

The Art of Being Ruled. London, Chatto and Windus, 1926.

The Enemy: A Review of Art and Literature, vol. 1, London, The Arthur Press, January 1927.

The Lion and the Fox. The Role of the Hero in the Plays of Shakespeare. London, Grant Richards, 1927. (London, Methuen, 1955).

Time and Western Man. London, Chatto and Windus, 1927.

The Wild Body: A Soldier of Humour and Other Stories. London, Chatto and Windus, 1927.

The Childermass: Section 1. London, Chatto and Windus, 1928. (London, Calder and Boyars, 1965.)

Tarr. London, Chatto and Windus, The Phoenix Library, 1928. Totally rewritten and revised. (Calder and Boyars, 1968.)

The Enemy, No. 3, London, The Arthur Press, January, 1929.

The Apes of God, London, The Arthur Press, 1930. (Harmondsworth, Penguin Books, 1965.)

Satire and Fiction, also "Have with You to Great Queen Street!" The History of a Rejected Review, by Roy Campbell. London, The Arthur Press, Enemy Pamphlets, No. 1. September 1930.

Hitler. London, Chatto and Windus, 1931.

The Diabolical Principle and the Dithyrambic Spectator. London, Chatto and Windus, 1931.

Doom of Youth. London, Chatto and Windus, 1932.

The Enemy of the Stars. London, Desmond Harmsworth, 1932.

Snooty Baronet. London, Cassell, 1932.

Filibusters in Barbary. New York, Robert M. McBride, 1932.

The Old Gang and the New Gang. London, Desmond Harmsworth, 1933.

One-Way Song. London, Faber and Faber, 1933.

Men without Art. London, Cassell, 1934.

"Studies in the Art of Laughter," *The London Mercury*, 30, No. 180 (October, 1934), 509–15.

Left Wings over Europe: or, How to Make a War about Nothing. London, Cape, 1936.

The Roaring Queen. London, Jonathan Cape, 1936. (Withdrawn before publication.)

The Revenge for Love. London, Cassell, 1937. (London, Methuen, 1952.)

Blasting and Bombardiering. London, Eyre and Spottiswoode, 1937. (Calder and Boyars, 1967.)

The Vulgar Streak. London, Robert Hale, 1941.

America and Cosmic Man. London, Nicolson and Watson, 1948.

Rude Assignment: A Narrative of My Career Up-to-date. London, Hutchinson, 1950.

"The Sea-Mists of the Winter," *The Listener*, 45, No. 1158. (May 10, 1951), 765.

Rotting Hill. London, Methuen, 1951.

The Writer and the Absolute. London, Methuen, 1952.

"The Rebellious Patient," *Shenandoah*, 4, Nos. 2–3 (Summer/Autumn, 1953), 3–16.

"Doppelgänger: A Story," *Encounter*, 2, No. 1 (January, 1954), 23–33.

Self Condemned. London, Methuen, 1954.

The Demon of Progress in the Arts. London, Methuen, 1954.

The Human Age. Book 2: Monstre Gai. Book 3. Malign Fiesta. London, Methuen, 1955. (Calder and Boyars, 1965.)

"Pish-Tush," *Encounter*, 6, No. 2 (February, 1956), 40–50.
The Red Priest. London, Methuen. 1956.

Secondary Sources

Agenda: (Wyndham Lewis Special Issue), Autumn–Winter 1969–70.

ALLEN, WALTER: "Lonely Old Volcano," *Encounter* 21, September 1963, 63–70.

BELL, Q. AND CHAPLIN, S: "The Ideal Home Rumpus," *Apollo*, October 1964, 284–91.

CAMPBELL, ROY: *Light on a Dark Horse*. London, 1951.

Canadian Literature: Special Lewis Edition (*Wyndham Lewis in Canada*), Vancouver, 1968.

ELIOT, T. S.: "A Note on Monstre Gai," *Hudson Review*, Winter 1955.

GRIGSON, G.: *A Master of Our Time*. London, 1951.

HOLLOWAY, J.: *The Charted Mirror*. London, 1960.

HOLROYD, MICHAEL: *Lytton Strachey*. London, 1967.

JOHN, AUGUSTUS: *Chiaroscuro*. London, 1952.

JOLAS, E. (et al): "First Aid to the Enemy," *transition* 9, December 1927, 160–176.

KENNER, HUGH: *Wyndham Lewis*. Norfolk, Conn., 1954.

MICHEL, W.: *Wyndham Lewis: Paintings and Drawings*. London, 1971.

MICHEL, W. AND FOX, C. J.: *Wyndham Lewis on Art*. London, 1969.

NEVINSON, C. R. W.: *Paint and Prejudice*. London, 1937.

PORTEUS, HUGH: *Wyndham Lewis: A Discursive Exposition*. London, 1932.

PRITCHARD, W. H.: *Wyndham Lewis*. New York, 1969.

ROSE, W. K. (Ed): *The Letters of Wyndham Lewis*. London, 1963.

ROSENTHAL, R. (Ed): *A Soldier of Humor and Selected Writings*. New York, 1966.

ROTHENSTEIN, JOHN: *British Art Since 1900*. London, 1962.

ROTHENSTEIN, JOHN: *Modern English Painters: Lewis to Moore*. London, 1962.

Shenandoah: (Wyndham Lewis Number) 4, Summer–Autumn, 1953.

SWINNERTON, FRANK: *The Georgian Literary Scene*. London, 1935.

TOMLIN, E. W. F.: *Wyndham Lewis*. London, 1955.

WAGNER, G.: *Wyndham Lewis: A Portrait of the Artist as the Enemy*. New Haven, 1957.

WEES, W. C.: "England's Avant-Garde: The Futurist-Vorticist Phase," *Western Humanities Review*, 21, 1967.

WOOLF, LEONARD: *Beginning Again*. London, 1965.

WOOLF, VIRGINIA: *Roger Fry*. London, 1940.

Index